As well as owning and running the world-famous Kinloch Lodge on the Isle of Skye for four decades, Claire Macdonald is the author of twenty best-selling cookery books and has appeared at cookery demonstrations worldwide. In recognition of her contribution to Scottish food, in 2011 she was presented with a Lifetime Achievement Award by the National Farmers' Union and the Royal Highland and Agricultural Society of Scotland. Claire was also awarded an honorary doctorate by Abertay University in 2008 and an OBE in 2014 for services to the food industry in Scotland and her work with Marie Curie Cancer Care.

THE
CLAIRE MACDONALD
GAME
COOKBOOK

Photography by Laurie Campbell

BIRLINN

For Philipp

First published in
Great Britain in 2015 by
Birlinn Ltd
West Newington House
10 Newington Road
Edinburgh
EH9 1QS

www.birlinn.co.uk

ISBN: 978 1 78027 283 2

British Library Cataloguing-in-Publication Data
A catalogue record for this book is available on request
from the British Library

Typeset and designed by Mark Blackadder

Printed and bound in Latvia by Livonia

CONTENTS

INTRODUCTION

Game, collectively speaking, is delicious. Yet the very word 'game' still strikes feelings of fear and foreboding into the hearts of too many people, for a variety of reasons. Within this book I fervently hope to dispel these misgivings, and to open the world of good eating that's to be discovered when game becomes a regular part of our diet during its autumn and winter season.

    This is a practical book. I abide by how I love to eat, and how I live my life – which is also how many others eat and live. I don't have time nor inclination to bone out a bird, for example. You won't find any recipes within this book asking you to do so. I go by the motto that life is too short to stuff a cherry – or to bone a gamebird! Nor will you find any way-out recipes here – there's no Pheasant Vindaloo, for example, or Casseroled Squirrel. But the reasons for just why game is still viewed with suspicion must be addressed. The first common misconception is that game is the prerogative of those who live in rural areas. Yet it is as accessible to those dwelling in the innermost areas of cities, sold through good butchers' shops, and most supermarkets sell several species of game, too. Pheasant is perhaps the easiest to access, because it is by far the most numerous of all the birds shot, and you can find it sold whole, or the breasts only, or what is described as 'fricassee', which is small chunks of the pheasant trimmings.

A close second misconception, and frequently encountered in mainland Europe too (where game is valued as a food to a far greater extent than it is in Britain), is that all game tastes strong. You can't judge all game this way, because it tastes so different! For instance, the very mildest of game birds are pheasant and red-legged partridge (as opposed to the grey-legged partridge, which for me is the greatest treat). Hanging game, both feathered and furred – and wild salmon too – is essential. How long to hang is weather dependent – for instance, grouse shot on a warm early autumn day will need about five days' hanging, whereas pheasant or any other game bird shot on a cold, frosty day will benefit from up to 10–14 days' hanging, and venison and wild boar can take even longer. But hanging is essential, both for texture and for flavour. Fortunately, however, the fashion for grouse hung for so long that they turned green and dropped from their hooks is over. Well-hung grouse is strong in taste. But it needn't be overpowering, providing that the hanging is for a judicial length of time, not too long.

I have always abided by eating food in its rightful season. This keeps the cook on his or her toes, and it prevents the palate from becoming jaded. Game is the perfect example: it should only ever be eaten in its season, which stretches from 12th August (for grouse) to the end of January. At the back of this book you will find a list of dates for both the feathered and furred game. These dates go back to 1831, when an Act of Parliament was passed to lay down laws necessary for game conservation. Incidentally, I read recently that these dates were lifted during the

First World War, to enable people to have access to a wider provision of food. I give myself and others a small licence of up to 14 days to use up frozen game birds after the end of January, although I know of one very dear friend who loathes eating pheasant once the season closes, even by one day. Game does freeze, venison as well as any other red meat, but game birds only freeze well for a limited time before deteriorating in both flavour and texture. This applies especially to some types of wild duck which, when frozen, can take on a fishy taste.

Some chapters in this book are short – woodcock and snipe, for example, and wild boar – while the lengthiest chapter is the pheasant recipes. But the first two chapters are slightly different. The first contains recipes using combinations of game. These recipes are so useful because they can be adapted according to what you might have at the time – for example if you buy or are given a hare, and you roast its saddle but have two back legs left over. Or if you buy some old grouse – which is delicious, but needs lengthy cooking. Rabbit (not in itself game but it, like pigeon, combines very well with all types of game), pheasant, and any type of game can be combined together in, for instance, a game pie. Or game soup. Or a game terrine. You don't have to have enough of just one type of game to concoct a hearty, sustaining and delicious game and root vegetable hot pot, nor a game salmis.

There's an all-important chapter on accompaniments for various types of game – some traditional, others less so, but they are included in the chapter because, being the greedy eater that I am, I find their taste and texture combinations with game utterly delicious. I think that accompaniments matter to everything we eat, but to game especially.

As the season wears on game becomes positively economical. Don't let your vision of such culinary bounty be clouded by erroneous visions of landlords, or shooting parties – an outdated notion. If you are swithering, then just think that with the sole exception of pheasant, all other game birds are a vital part of the conservation of our moorlands and woods. And keeping the land is not only a valued form of employment in rural areas, but also an essential part of maintaining the balance of our countryside.

I hope with all my heart that this book proves to be a useful source of recipes as well as giving the nudge needed by some to buy some game, cook it, eat it and see just how delicious it is, as well as being a superb form of nutrition. Versatile and convenient, with game the message above all others is – enjoy!

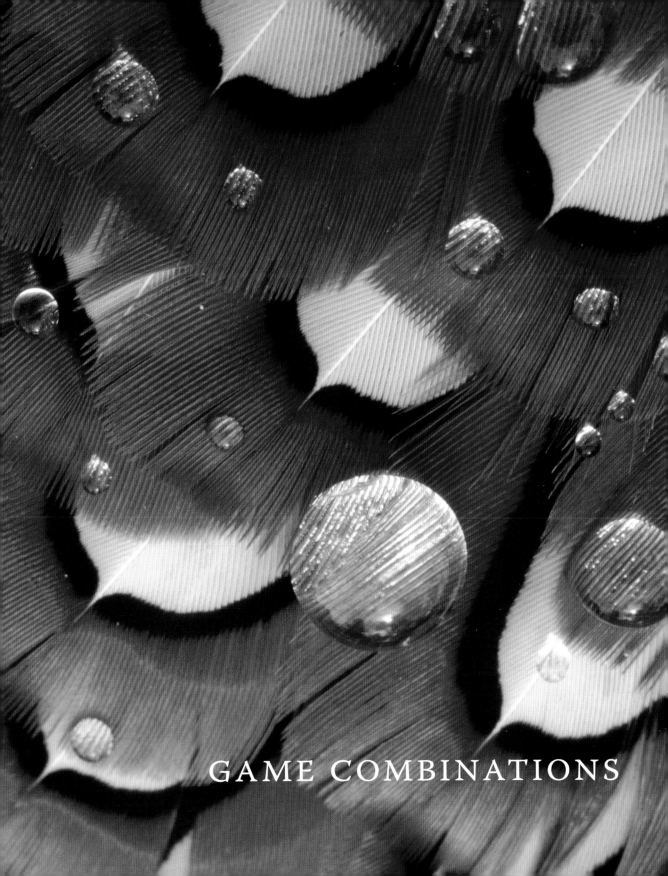

GAME COMBINATIONS

Game Pie

A good game pie makes the most wonderful dish for a special lunch with family and friends. It ticks all the boxes. It's convenient in that it can be made in its entirety 24 hours ahead, needing only to be baked before serving. And the forcemeat balls (see p.21) can be made, shallow fried and frozen, then thawed and reheated in an ovenproof dish loosely covered with foil, to serve with the game pie.

For game pie I prefer to use puff pastry, and I buy this rather than making my own. But some brands are better than others. If you can't find the excellent Bells brand, then use any other all-butter puff pastry.

Put the stock and thyme sprig into a saucepan and bring to simmering point. Simmer with the pan uncovered until the stock has reduced by half.

Meanwhile, mix the salt and pepper and freshly grated nutmeg into the flour, then put this into a large polythene bag. Add the chunks of game meat. Shake the bag vigorously, to coat each chunk of meat in the seasoned flour.

Heat the oil in a large casserole and brown the floured game chunks, a small amount at a time, making sure it is browned on all sides. Scoop the meat into a warm dish, leaving behind as much oil as you can, before adding more game chunks to the casserole.

When all the game is browned, reduce the heat slightly beneath the casserole and fry the diced onions, stirring occasionally, until they are soft and transparent, about 5 minutes.

Scrape the bits off the base of the casserole, and stir in the wine and the reduced stock – fish out the thyme and chuck it in the bin – stirring until the liquid bubbles. Stir in the Worcestershire sauce and the redcurrant or bramble jelly.

Serves 6

1.2 litres / 2½ pints game stock (see recipe on p.5) or shop-bought chicken stock

1 sprig of thyme

1kg / 2¼lb game (e.g. pheasant, old grouse, hare, rabbit) cut into 2cm / 1" chunks and trimmed of any gristle, skin and sinew

2 rounded tbsp flour

1 tsp salt, about 20 grinds black pepper, a grating of nutmeg

4 tbsp olive or rapeseed oil

2 onions, skinned and finely diced (use 3 banana shallots if you prefer a slightly milder taste)

1 fat clove of garlic, skinned and finely diced

150ml / ¼ pint full-bodied red wine – e.g. merlot or sangiovese

1 tbsp Lea & Perrins Worcestershire sauce*

2 tsp redcurrant or bramble jelly

500g / 1lb puff pastry

1 large egg, beaten well

* Only Lea & Perrins will do, because it contains the vital ingredient of anchovy, which other makes of Worcestershire sauce omit from their recipes.

When the sauce is simmering, put the browned game back into the casserole, stir it into the sauce, and bring the liquid back to a gentle simmer. Cover the casserole with its lid and cook in a moderate oven (180°C / 350°F / gas 4) for 1 hour.

Take the casserole out of the oven and, when cool, spoon the contents into a pie dish. This can be done up to 48 hours before baking the pie, but be sure to cover the pie dish and its contents with clingfilm and store it in the fridge.

Roll out the puff pastry on a lightly floured board to a size large enough to more than cover the surface of the pie dish. Roll the pastry loosely around your rolling pin when you have finished rolling it out – this makes it is much easier to lay over the surface of the pie filling without tearing the pastry with your fingers.

To complete the pie, take the pie dish from the fridge. Put a couple of eggcups or ceramic pie birds into the contents, pushing them down, to support the pastry. Brush the edges of the dish with beaten egg, then cover the entire dish with the rolled-out puff pastry. Trim it around the edges with a sharp knife, leaving a very small overhang (the pastry will shrink slightly as it cooks).

Shape the edges of the pastry, either by pinching the pastry together at neat, repeated intervals, or, using the blunt edge of the blade of a small knife, at regular intervals and close together cut into the pastry edge.*

Brush the entire surface of the pastry with beaten egg. Slash it evenly in about 8 places to let the steam escape during cooking time. Any leftover pastry can be artistically shaped into leaves or roses – use your imagination! (Or leave it plain: unadorned but golden brown puff pastry looks very good to me.)

Bake the game pie in a hot oven (200°C / 400°F / gas 6) for 20 minutes, then reduce the heat to moderate (180°C / 350°F / gas 4) and cook the pie for a further 20–25 minutes, or until the pastry is well puffed up and deeply golden in colour.

Serve with rowan and apple jelly (see recipe on p.27) handed separately, and with forcemeat balls.

* I once saw a seaside postcard, many years ago, depicting a woman using her set of false teeth to make an intriguing edge to her pie, but I am certainly not advocating that you should try this!

Game Stock

There are only two items to leave out of all stock – and game stock is no exception – and they are turnip and potato. Both these root vegetables turn a stock sour. It is hard to beat good game stock. Make a good batch, 3–4 litres, then simmer the stock to reduce it by half. This intensifies its flavour. But we are all limited in the amount of space we have in our freezers. I have discovered that the most space efficient way to freeze stock is in cylindrical plastic bottles, but the least efficient containers are bowls. ALWAYS label the bottles with the contents and date of making – it is alarming how quickly items take on anonymity once frozen. Start the stock in a large roasting tin, then use your biggest pan or casserole.

4 carcases, from any game bird (if you are using venison too, cut it into large chunks, bones and all)

4 tbsp olive or rapeseed oil

3 onions, quartered, skin and all (the skin gives a rich, dark colour)

1 head of celery, washed, dried and chopped into large chunks

4 carrots, washed, dried and cut into chunks

3 leeks, washed, dried and cut into chunks

2 tsp black peppercorns, crushed in a mortar and pestle

3 juniper berries, crushed with the end of your rolling pin

Pared rind of 1 washed and dried orange (use a sharp potato peeler, to avoid any bitter white pith)

2–3l / 3½–5 pints cold water

Add 2 tsp salt once stock is cooked

Put the game carcases (and venison if using) into the roasting tin with the chopped vegetables, bashed peppercorns and juniper berries, and the olive or rapeseed oil. Mix all together, so that everything has a fine coating of oil, then roast in a hot oven (200°C / 400°F / gas 6) for 40–45 minutes. During this time, open the oven and shake the roasting tin once or twice to move around the contents.

Take the roasting tin out of the oven and pour in the water, then tip the contents into a large pan or casserole. Bring the water in the pan to a simmer, cover the pan and cook, simmering gently, for 2 hours.

Take the pan off the heat, cool the contents, then strain into a smaller pan. Discard the carcases, meat and vegetables. Put the pan on the heat and simmer, the pan uncovered, until reduced by half in quantity. Cool, then pour the concentrated cold stock into containers. Seal, label and freeze.

Game Soup

Serves 6

50g / 2oz butter

2 rashers unsmoked top-quality back bacon, trimmed of fat (easiest done using scissors) then sliced into thin strips

220g / 8oz lamb's liver, trimmed of membranes and chopped

2 medium onions, skinned and finely chopped

1 carrot, peeled and chopped

2 potatoes (approx. 220g / 8oz), peeled and chopped

1 garlic clove, peeled and chopped

1 litre / 2 pints game stock (see recipe on p.5)

150 ml / ¼ pint port

1 tsp redcurrant jelly

2 strips pared orange rind and 1 strip pared lemon rind (use a sharp potato peeler, to avoid any bitter white pith)

1 rounded tsp salt, about 15 grinds black pepper

1 rounded tbsp finely chopped parsley – to stir through the soup just before serving

Game soup can be positively deadly, but with the unexpected inclusion of a small amount of lamb's liver and using excellent game stock, this version is a winner. But I have always tried to give credit to those who inspire me, and I can't claim that the lamb's liver is my own brilliant discovery: it's not. This ingenious addition is entirely down to one of Britain's best food writers of all time, the late Katie Stewart, whose brilliant recipes are her legacy.

Melt the butter in a large saucepan and fry the strips of bacon and the lamb's liver, stirring, for 2–3 minutes, then scoop them on to a plate. Add the chopped onions and carrots to the pan and cook, stirring occasionally, until the onions are soft and transparent, about 5 minutes.

Add the chopped potatoes and garlic, stir well, and pour in the stock, port, redcurrant jelly, orange and lemon rinds, salt and black pepper. Stir well and, pan uncovered, bring the liquid to a gentle simmering point. Half-cover the pan with its lid and cook gently for 25–30 minutes, or until the vegetables are tender.

When the soup has cooled, add the fried bacon and liver to the contents of the pan. Liquidise until smooth. Taste and adjust the seasoning if necessary.

Reheat before serving, with the finely chopped parsley stirred through the hot soup just before ladling it into soup plates to serve.

Game Pudding

This is one of the most richly satisfying ways to serve game. Don't for one moment think that the words 'suet crust' indicate imminent death via hardened arteries — these days we can buy reduced-fat suet, which makes a good substitute for the real thing. A steamed suet crust, containing a subtle hint of lemon and thyme, is an unctuous dish. This pudding is greatly enhanced by a green vegetable such as Brussels sprouts or stir-fried cabbage, and also by roast root vegetables, but potatoes are not necessary an accompaniment.

For the suet crust

In a bowl mix together the flour, suet, lemon rind, thyme, salt and black pepper, stirring in just enough of the cold water to bind the ingredients together.

On a floured surface roll out two thirds of the dough and line a plastic boilable pudding bowl (1.7 litre / 3 pint capacity) with the suet pastry. The pastry won't fill the bowl to the brim, don't worry.

Roll out the remaining third of the dough in a disc just bigger than the lid of the pudding bowl. Set to one side.

For the filling

Put the game meat into a bowl and add the seasoned flour and the shallots. With your hands, mix it all together thoroughly.

Put the water and red wine into a saucepan and add the redcurrant jelly. Over moderate heat dissolve the jelly in the liquid. Take the pan off the heat and cool.

Pack the seasoned and floured game meat and shallots into the pastry-lined pudding bowl. Pour in the liquid, carefully easing it

Serves 6

For the suet crust

375g / 12oz self-raising flour

175g / 6oz suet (can be reduced-fat version)

Finely grated rind of 1 lemon

Pinch of dried thyme leaves

1 level tsp salt, about 10 grinds of black pepper

About 150ml / ¼ pint cold water

For the filling

1kg / 2lb assorted game meat — e.g. venison, old grouse, pheasant, hare — cut into equal-sized chunks

2 level tbsp flour mixed with 1 tsp salt and 20 grinds black pepper

2 banana shallots, skinned, halved and finely diced

600ml / 1 pint water/red wine (I make it half and half)

2 tsp redcurrant jelly

amongst the game. Cover the contents with the rolled-out suet pastry disc, and pinch it together with the pastry lining the bowl. Put a disc of baking parchment on top, and snap the lid on to the pudding bowl. Put the pudding bowl into a large saucepan and pour in boiling water, to come halfway up the sides of the bowl. On moderate heat bring the water in the pan to a gentle simmer, cover the pan with its lid, and simmer gently, the water just simmering, for 4½–5 hours. Set your timer and check the water level in the pan regularly, topping it up with boiling water from the kettle whenever it is required. Be vigilant! Nothing is sadder than a game pudding which has been forgotten during its lengthy cooking time, the plastic bowl as one with the base of the pan in which it was cooking. Keep checking the water!

Before serving, have a jug of hot port-flavoured game stock to hand, for pouring into the opened game pudding, because the suet pastry will absorb much of the liquid that was added to the contents of the pudding before cooking. Mix 900ml / 1½ pints reduced game stock with 150ml / ¼ pint port in a saucepan and simmer together for 2–3 minutes, then pour into a Thermos jug. When the pudding is cooked, take the lid off the bowl, throw away the parchment disc, and serve the pudding, pouring over some of the game and port stock.

Game Pasty

A game pasty makes a perfect picnic for a day out hiking during cold winter weeks. These pasties can be made a day in advance, then popped into the oven to bake on the morning of the excursion, and loosely and individually wrapped in greaseproof paper once cooked. If you like, wrap the paper-wrapped pasties in foil, but avoid wrapping the baked hot pasty itself directly in foil: the pastry deteriorates as it cools.

Put the trimmed game meat into a food processor and whiz briefly, to pulverise to the consistency of coarse mince (take care not to make a puree of the meat).

In a casserole heat the olive oil and brown the minced game meat thoroughly, then scoop the browned mixture into a warm dish.

Add the onions, carrots and leek to the casserole and cook, stirring occasionally, for 6–8 minutes. Add the garlic and the browned game meat, mix well, and stir in the flour. Cook for a minute before adding the stock, tomato puree, redcurrant jelly, Worcestershire sauce, salt and black pepper.

Cook until the contents of the casserole reach simmering point, then cover the casserole with its lid and cook in a moderate oven (180°C / 350°F / gas 4) for 1 hour. When the cooking time is up, take the casserole out of the oven and cool the contents.

To make the pasties – and mine are oblong, not traditional pasty shapes (I find it more economical to cut the rolled-out pastry into rectangles rather than circles, and simpler, too!) – roll out the pastry on a lightly floured work surface. You may find it easier to do this in two batches, depending on the size of your surface. Trim the pastry and cut into 6 even-sized rectangles.

Serves 6

675g / 1½lb shortcrust pastry

1 large egg, beaten

For the filling

675g / 1½lb assorted game meat, trimmed of sinew or membrane

2–3 tbsp olive or rapeseed oil

2 medium onions, skinned and finely diced

2 carrots, peeled and finely diced

1 leek, outer leaves removed, then trimmed and sliced finely

1 fat clove of garlic, skinned and neatly diced

1 rounded tbsp flour

600ml / 1 pint game stock (or good chicken stock)

1 tbsp tomato puree

2 tsp redcurrant jelly

1 tbsp Lea & Perrins Worcestershire sauce

1 tsp salt, about 15 grinds black pepper

Brush the edges of each rectangle with beaten egg. Spoon a sixth of the cooled game mixture on to one side of each rectangle. Fold over the other part of the pastry rectangle and press it firmly on to the egg-washed rim of the filling side. With your two thumbs, pinch together the pastry all around the rim. Put the pasties on a metal baking sheet, then brush each pasty all over with beaten egg. Bake in a hot oven (200°C / 400°F / gas 6) for 15 minutes, then drop the heat to moderate (180°C / 350°F / gas 4) and bake for a further 20–25 minutes. Check the pasties during cooking, and don't let the pastry become too dark in colour.

When cooked, leave the pasties on the baking tray for a minute, then carefully loosen them, using a metal spatula.

Salmis of Game

I was taught by my aunt, who worked at the Cordon Bleu with Rosemary Hume and Constance Spry, that a salmis was a combination of two methods of cooking: a brief roasting time then braising. I find this method of cooking odds and ends of assorted game very useful, even if the roasting tin looks a bit strange with a couple of partridge, a pheasant and a hare leg, for example, at its initial stage of cooking! Prepare whatever assortment of game you are using in your salmis carefully. This is a game dish I always accompany with forcemeat balls.

For the roast birds

Put the shallots into a roasting tin and place the birds on top. Lay the bacon rashers loosely over the top of the birds – no need to cover each bird individually. Grind black pepper over it all.

Roast in a hot oven (200°C / 400°F / gas 6) for 20 minutes, then take the roasting tin out of the oven and cool.

When cold, cut the meat from the carcases into large chunks. Keep any juices from the birds to add to the casserole for braising.

For the sauce

Start by roasting the mushrooms – put the diced mushrooms and the 2 tablespoons of olive oil on to a small roasting tin. Mix the oil thoroughly through the mushrooms, spread them in an even layer and roast them in the oven, with or after the game, at the same temperature, for 30–35 minutes. Remove from the oven and scoop the roasted mushrooms into a bowl, leaving behind as much of the olive oil as you can.

Serves 6

For the roast birds

Enough game to serve 6 – e.g. 1 cock pheasant, 2 partridge, 2 mallard

8 rashers top-quality streaky bacon

2 banana shallots, skinned and halved lengthways

Black pepper

For the sauce

1 tbsp olive or rapeseed oil

25g / 1oz butter

3 banana shallots, skinned and finely diced

2 sticks celery, trimmed and peeled with a potato peeler to remove the stringy bits, then sliced as finely as possible

450g / 1lb flat mushrooms, wiped and stalks cut level with the caps, then the caps cut into large dice

2 tbsp olive oil

1 rounded tbsp flour

600ml / 1 pint reduced game stock (or good chicken stock)

150ml / ¼ pint port

Small sprig of thyme (or a pinch of dried thyme leaves)

1 tsp salt, about 20 grinds black pepper

Heat the remaining tablespoon of oil and butter together in a casserole, and fry the shallots and celery, stirring from time to time, over a moderately high heat for about 5 minutes. Stir in the flour and cook for a couple of minutes before gradually adding the reduced game stock and the port. Stir until the sauce simmers gently. Add the sprig of thyme, the salt and black pepper and stir in the roast mushrooms. Add the chunks of semi-roasted game and bring the sauce back to simmering before covering the casserole with its lid. Cook in a moderate oven (180°C / 350°F / gas 4) for 45 minutes.

This is good served with mashed celeriac and potatoes, and with a green vegetable, such as Brussels sprouts, kale, spinach or cabbage.

Game Terrine

This makes a wonderful first course, and is delicious served with Cumberland jelly and a salad dressed with a mustardy vinaigrette, perfect before a fish main course. But this terrine can be a very good main course, served with salad and baked jacket potatoes, and accompanied by chutney. It is so convenient in that it has to be made at least 24 hours ahead.

Start by making the marinade. Put all the ingredients for the marinade into a saucepan over moderate heat and simmer gently for 5 minutes, then take the pan off the heat and cool the contents completely. When cold, discard the strips of orange rind.

Line a metal loaf tin with foil, carefully easing it into each corner.

Put each streaky bacon rasher onto a board and, using the blade of a knife, elongate each by stroking down the rasher. You can made the rashers half as long again by doing this.

Put the bay leaves on the foil. Lay the bacon rashers over the width of the tin, easing them down to line it, so that the ends of each rasher overlap at either edge.

Put the diced game meat and skinned pork sausages into a mixing bowl, add the salt and black pepper and the cold marinade. With your hand – there is no other way to do this thoroughly – squidge it all together. Then put this mixture into the bacon-lined tin, pressing it down. Flip the edges of the bacon rashers over and fold the foil over.

Put the terrine into a roasting tin and pour boiling water to come halfway up the side of the tin. Cook in a moderate oven (180°C / 350°F / gas 4) for 2–2½ hours.

Serves 8 as a first course or 6 as a main course

For the marinade

4 tbsp olive oil (use olive rather than rapeseed oil for this)

150ml / ¼ pint red wine

2 medium onions, skinned and finely diced (rough chopping will not do, because the whole marinade becomes a part of the terrine)

3–4 juniper berries, bashed with the end of a rolling pin

Pared rind of 1 orange

For the terrine

675g / 1½lb game meat, evenly diced into thumbnail-sized pieces

450g / 1lb top-quality pork sausages, skins removed

1 tsp salt, 15 grinds black pepper

For preparing the terrine tin

12–14 slices top-quality streaky bacon

3 bay leaves

Take the roasting tin and terrine out of the oven, put a weight on top – try a couple of tins of tomatoes – and leave to cool completely. Then remove the weights, lift the terrine out of the roasting tin, dry its base with kitchen paper and store in the fridge for up to 2 days, until you are ready to serve.

To serve, invert on to a serving plate, lift off the tin, peel off the foil, and cut into 1cm slices.

NB: This terrine does not freeze successfully once cooked – it crumbles when thawed and sliced. However, it does freeze well when made in its entirety but not cooked. Take it out of the freezer 36 hours ahead of cooking, and to be sure it is thawed, unwrap the foil and stick your finger into the middle to feel for any icy particles. If there are any, cook it for an extra 45 minutes.

Game and Root Vegetable Hot Pot

This is reminiscent of a Lancashire hot pot, but made with game and containing, I think, a more interesting amalgamation of root vegetables. The beetroot in the recipe helps to tenderise the game, although the lengthy cooking time should take care of that itself! This is the only recipe for game in this book for which the game meat isn't browned or roasted; instead it is blanched and layered up with the vegetables. It is a hearty and delicious dish, packed with nutrition. It also has the benefit of being a meal in one pot.

Put the game meat into a pan and cover with cold water. Over heat, bring the water to simmering point, then drain off the water and rinse the game.

Put the prepared vegetables into a large bowl and mix well.

Put the water, salt, pepper, bashed juniper berries and redcurrant jelly into a small saucepan over heat, until the jelly has melted.

In a large, wide ovenproof dish or casserole put half the vegetable mixture, then put the blanched game meat in an even layer over this, and cover with the remainder of the vegetables. Finally, arrange the sliced potatoes over the entire surface. Lastly, pour the flavoured and seasoned water over and into the contents.

Cover the surface with baking parchment and put the lid on top of that, and cook in a low-moderate heat (150°C / 300°F / gas 3) for 3¾–4 hours. It will keep warm for longer, but in a much cooler oven. Serve.

NB: The vegetables will make their own juices during cooking time, so when you look into the cooking pot, don't be surprised to find more liquid than you initially put in!

Serves 6

1kg / 2lb game meat, of any combination, cut into even-sized chunks (approx. 2cm / 1")

4 onions, skinned and finely sliced

3 beetroot, peeled and sliced into fat matchsticks

3 carrots, peeled, trimmed and sliced into fat matchsticks

3 parsnips, peeled, trimmed and sliced into fat matchsticks

3 medium leeks, outer leaves removed, trimmed and sliced fairly thinly

2 fat cloves garlic, skinned and finely sliced

600ml / 1 pint cold water

2 tsp salt, about 20 grinds black pepper

3 juniper berries, bashed with the end of a rolling pin

2 tsp redcurrant jelly

Potted Game with Walnuts

Serves 6

120g / 4oz walnuts, chopped

2 tbsp olive oil

1 tsp salt, 15 grinds black pepper

2 juniper berries, bashed using the end of a rolling pin

375g / 12oz leftover roast game meat, from any species of bird (discard all membrane, sinews and, of course, even the smallest bones)

175g / 6oz butter

2 cloves garlic, blanched

2 tbsp Lea & Perrins Worcestershire sauce

This is one recipe for which you won't have a combination of game meats, because it is made using leftover roast game, but you can make this recipe using any of the game birds. It is a wonderful way to use up a fairly small amount of roast game bird, to serve as a first course, and can be made up to two days before eating. Don't be alarmed about clarifying butter – it's so easy, and very worthwhile. The result is rich and succulent, and the smooth texture contrasts well with the crunch of the fried walnuts.

Start by putting the butter into a small saucepan in a warm place – on the back of a Raeburn or Aga, or on top of a radiator, but not on direct heat. Let the butter melt, very slowly.

Heat the olive oil in a frying or sauté pan and fry the chopped walnuts, with the salt and black pepper, for 5–7 minutes, stirring from time to time. Take the pan off the heat and cool the nuts.

To blanch the garlic cloves in their skins, immerse them in cold water in a small saucepan. Bring the water to the boil. Drain and repeat. Cut the ends off each clove of garlic, and the skin peels off easily.

Put the game meat, garlic and Worcestershire sauce into a food processor and briefly whiz. Tip into a mixing bowl and mix in the cooled walnuts.

Carefully pour half the melted butter into the contents of the bowl – by pouring carefully the milky curd remains at the base of the pan; the clear liquid on top is the clarified butter. You will need the remaining butter to seal the potted game.

Mix the butter thoroughly into the game and walnut mixture, then divide this evenly between 6 small containers. Carefully pour the remaining clarified butter over the surface of each little pot.

Cool, cover each pot with clingfilm, and store in the fridge until you are ready to serve. I particularly like to serve this with Melba toast.

Game with Oatmeal Crumble

This oatmeal crumble makes such a delicious alternative to pastry or mashed potatoes or any other root vegetables. The crumble uses porridge (rolled) oats, and is convenient because it can be made a couple of days ahead of time. I think the crumble is as interesting as the mixture it covers – the flavours of fried diced onion, thyme and lemon are deliciously complementary to the game underneath.

Put the game meat into a large ziplock bag with the flour, salt and black pepper. Close the bag and shake it hard to coat the chunks of meat with seasoned flour.

Heat the oil in a casserole or stew pan. Brown the floured chunks of game on all sides, removing it as it browns to a warm dish. Lower the heat slightly beneath the pan and add the onion, carrots and celery. Fry over moderate heat, stirring occasionally, for 8–10 minutes.

Add the lager, stock and tomato puree, scraping the base of the pan, and stir until the sauce simmers.

Add the browned game, mix well, and bring the sauce back to a simmer. Cover the pan with its lid and cook in a moderate oven (180°C / 350°F / gas 4) for 1 hour. Take the pan out of the oven and cool the contents.

Meanwhile, make the crumble by heating the oil and frying the diced onion over a moderately high heat for 4–5 minutes, until soft and transparent. Take the pan off the heat.

Serves 6

For the crumble

2 tbsp olive or rapeseed oil

1 medium onion, skinned and finely diced

Finely grated rind of 1 lemon

A small sprig of fresh thyme, or a pinch of dried thyme leaves

1 tsp salt, about 10 grinds black pepper

175g / 6oz porridge oats

50g / 2oz reduced-fat suet

For the game mixture

900g / 2lb game meat –
e.g. pheasant, partridge, hare, venison
– cut into 2cm / 1" chunks, using any
combination of odds and ends of
game you have

2 level tbsp flour

1 tsp salt, 20 grinds black pepper

3 tbsp olive or rapeseed oil

2 onions, skinned and neatly diced

2 carrots, peeled and neatly diced

3 sticks celery, trimmed and peeled
with a potato peeler to remove the
stringy bits, and then finely sliced

1 tbsp tomato puree

1 can lager

300ml / ½ pint stock (use chicken
stock or a good substitute such as
Marigold stock powder)

In a bowl, combine the porridge oats, suet, finely grated lemon rind, thyme, salt and black pepper and mix in the fried onion and oil from the frying pan. Mix very thoroughly.

When the contents of the casserole are cold, scatter the oatmeal crumble evenly over the surface. Reheat by cooking in a moderate oven (180°C / 350°F / gas 4) for 40–45 minutes. The oatmeal crumble should be golden brown and the game bubbling gently around the edges.

NB: If you put the casserole straight from the fridge into the oven, allow an extra 30 minutes' cooking time.

SAUCES, STUFFINGS
AND ACCOMPANIMENTS

In this chapter are recipes for the jellies, sauces and vegetable concoctions which really enhance game dishes. For instance, forcemeat balls are so delicious with game pie, game salmis – in fact with pretty much any other game recipe. They are so convenient, as they can be made in advance and frozen, and I think forcemeat balls make potatoes unnecessary, but the final decision is yours, of course. There's a recipe for a proper game gravy – an essential accompaniment. Bread sauce is one of the classic sauces, but it must be well made, and in recipes it is rare to read what matters most, that the right bread must be used – a baked loaf, never a steamed, sliced loaf which gives the sauce a glue-like consistency. And the same applies to any recipe using white or brown breadcrumbs: the crumbs must be from a baked loaf.

In this chapter you'll find a recipe for a marinade. Every bit of game would benefit from being marinated, for the sake of imparting more flavour, but in some cases there is need for a marinade to both tenderise and raw out any strong flavours. For this purpose there is a one-item marinade – simply, milk. But the milk must be proper milk (i.e. full milk, not skimmed) and once the overnight marinating is over, you have to drain off the milk, which looks rather horrifically bloody by now.

Cumberland jelly and rowan and apple jelly both make terrific accompaniments to game. I always put apples into my rowan jelly, to lift the bitter flavour of the rowan berries.

Forcemeat Balls

Start by heating the tablespoon of oil and fry the onion, stirring, for 3–4 minutes.

In a bowl, mix the parsley breadcrumbs with the lemon rind, suet, salt and black pepper and the fried onion. Stir in the beaten egg and mix it all together thoroughly.

Scoop out of the bowl about two teaspoons of the mixture and roll into a small ball (I make them golf-ball size) between the palms of your hands. Roll this in sieved plain flour and put the balls onto a plastic tray lined with baking parchment until you have used up all the mixture.

Heat a small amount of oil – a couple of tablespoons – in a non-stick frying or sauté pan and, over moderately high heat, fry the forcemeat balls, carefully turning them until they are light golden-brown all over.

Line a roasting tin with three layers of absorbent kitchen paper and, as the forcemeat balls are cooked, lift them out of the pan and on to the kitchen paper. Cool.

When cold, pack the forcemeat balls into a solid polythene box. Label and freeze.

Allow 3 hours to thaw, taking them out of the box and placing onto a baking tray to thaw. Reheat in a moderate oven (180°C / 350°F / gas 4) for 15–20 minutes, then keep them warm at a lower temperature until you are ready to serve.

Serves 6

1 tbsp olive or rapeseed oil

1 onion, skinned and very finely diced

175g / 6oz fresh white breadcrumbs, made from a baked loaf, the bread pulverised in a food processor with a handful of parsley, tough stalks removed

75g / 3oz suet (can be the reduced-fat variety)

Finely grated rind of 1 lemon

1 large egg, beaten well

1 tsp salt, about 10 grinds black pepper

1 tbsp plain flour, sieved on to a plate, for coating the forcemeat balls

Oil for frying the forcemeat balls in a non-stick frying or sauté pan

Bread Sauce

Serves 6

1 onion, skinned and stuck with
12 cloves

1 stick of celery broken in two

900ml / 1½ pints milk

175g / 6oz freshly whizzed
breadcrumbs

1 tsp salt, about 15 grinds black
pepper, a good grating of nutmeg

50g / 2oz butter

It is perhaps not commonly known that bread sauce freezes exceptionally well. But there are two imperatives: that it must be made using breadcrumbs from a baked (not steamed) loaf, and that whole milk must be used, not skimmed.

Put the clove-stuck onion, celery and milk into a saucepan over a gentle to moderate heat. Be careful not to do this over too high a heat – the milk shouldn't boil. When a skin has formed, take the pan off the heat and leave it in a cool place. As the milk cools, so it becomes infused with the flavours of the cloves, onion and celery.

When the milk is cold, scoop out the onion and celery. Stir in the breadcrumbs, salt, pepper and nutmeg and reheat the milk – don't worry about the skin, as it will soon stir into the milk and breadcrumbs as it heats.

Add the butter and cook the sauce gently. Serve the bread sauce hot. It keeps warm in a low-temperature oven, providing the dish is covered, for up to an hour without spoiling.

Butter and Parsley-fried Breadcrumbs

Fried breadcrumbs are a traditional accompaniment to game birds such as roast grouse, but are also very good served with roast partridge and roast pheasant. I add parsley to the torn chunks of baked white bread before whizzing them to crumbs, which gives a good flavour. Now that we know butter is not bad for us, do not stint on the quality of the butter you use for frying, but don't do this over a high heat because butter burns at a lower heat than oil. The taste of buttery fried crumbs is delicious, and they keep warm very well without spoiling.

Melt the butter in a wide pan, ideally a sauté pan, over moderately high heat. Watch the heat, and don't let it get too hot. The butter mustn't brown.

Stir in the salt and the parsley breadcrumbs. Fry, stirring from time to time, so that the breadcrumbs become golden-brown and crisp all over.

Scoop the fried crumbs onto a warm dish lined with a couple of thicknesses of kitchen paper, to absorb the excess melted butter.

Serves 6

120g / 4oz butter

1 tsp salt

220g / 8oz baked bread (crusts removed), whizzed in a processor with 1 handful of parsley, all stalks discarded

Braised Red Cabbage with Shallots and Apples

Serves 6

2 onions, skinned and sliced thinly

3 tbsp olive or rapeseed oil

450g / 1lb red cabbage, hard white core removed and cabbage sliced thinly

2 eating apples, peeled, cored and chopped

½ tsp powdered cinnamon

1 tsp salt, about 20 grinds black pepper

300ml / ½ pint unsweetened apple juice

1 tsp balsamic vinegar

This is the only vegetable recipe in this chapter, and I include it because it is supremely complementary to a variety of game, whether roasted or casseroled. There is a peculiar affinity between red cabbage and game. This recipe is convenient too, as it can be made a day in advance, and it reheats very well without deteriorating. There is a tiny amount of cinnamon in the ingredients, but don't be tempted to add more, because although cinnamon is a wonderful spice it can take over the flavour if used in excess.

Heat the oil in a casserole or stew pan and fry the onions, stirring occasionally, for 5 minutes or until the onions are soft and transparent. Add the sliced red cabbage and chopped apples, the cinnamon, salt and black pepper. Stir in the apple juice and the balsamic vinegar. Mix all together well, and cover the pan with its lid. Cook over a moderate heat, lifting the lid and stirring the contents from time to time, for about 30 minutes. When the thickest slice of red cabbage feels tender when stuck with a fork, the dish is cooked. Either cool, and reheat gently before serving, or keep the casserole hot until you are ready to serve.

Cumberland Jelly

This is worth making just for one dish – it is that delicious! It's also worth doubling up the recipe and storing the finished jelly in the fridge for another time. This is just as good with roast venison as it is with roast wild duck, or with a game pie, or with game terrine . . . I could go on and on.

220g / 8oz redcurrant jelly

1 tsp mustard powder

150ml / ¼ pint port

2 leaves of gelatine soaked in cold water for 10 minutes

Finely grated rind and juice of 1 orange

Finely grated rind and juice of 1 lemon

In a saucepan mix the port and mustard powder, working them together, then add the redcurrant jelly to the pan and, over heat, melt the jelly.

Meanwhile, in another small pan heat the orange and lemon rinds and juice. Lift the soaked gelatine leaves from the cold water, dripping off as much water as possible, drop the gelatine into the hot orange and lemon liquids and swirl the pan to dissolve the gelatine. Then stir the contents of this saucepan into the redcurrant jelly mixture, stirring all together very well.

Pour into a clean, warmed pot. Cool, cover the pot with its lid, and store in the fridge until you are ready to serve it to accompany any type of game you choose.

Game Chips

Serves 6

Oil for deep-frying

3 medium potatoes, peeled and sliced very, very thinly (use a mandolin for the finest slicing)

Wafer-thin sliced potatoes deep-fried until golden brown are a traditional accompaniment to roast game birds of all varieties – except for wild duck. It is too easy to buy bags of crisps, warm up the contents and serve them instead, and of course we all do this from time to time. But, homemade, these potato 'chips' are so very much better. It is vital to start with a good variety of potato, not some anonymous spud. I go for Rooster, which as far as I am concerned is the best all-rounder, for flavour as well as for performance, whether roast or mashed or for making into game chips. And no, I am not a member of the board of potato growers! I speak purely from experience and awareness of the different varieties of the potato. These game chips can be made ahead by several hours, and warmed up before serving. Don't be afraid of deep frying. Use clean oil – I use sunflower oil – and fry in a small, deep pan.

Soak the sliced potatoes in cold water – this allows the starch to seep from the potatoes. Pat the slices dry, very thoroughly, between kitchen paper.

Heat clean oil (I never use it twice) to a depth of 6cm /3" and drop in a bit of bread to test the heat – the bit of bread should sizzle and turn golden within a few seconds. Remove it. Then fry the potato slices, turning them over, in batches. As they become golden brown, lift them onto a dish lined with a couple of thicknesses of kitchen paper. Scatter a small amount of salt over the cooked potato chips. Keep them warm in a low-temperature oven, uncovered, and serve in a warmed dish, having discarded the kitchen paper beneath them.

Rowan and Apple Jelly

This goes well with all roast game, but I think it is best with venison and wild boar. Adding the chopped eating apples to the berries gives a better depth of flavour to the jelly, and it also very slightly detracts from their bitterness. A great part of the appeal of this jelly is its bright, clear, orange-jewel appearance.

Put the berries and chopped apples into a large saucepan and cover with cold water. Bring to a simmer, and half-cover the pan. Cook until the berries are soft. This should take 25–30 minutes at a gentle simmer.

Take the pan off the heat and cool the contents. When cold, strain the liquid by tipping the contents into a large colander lined with muslin. Alternatively, strain through a jelly bag into a large bowl or a measuring jug. Leave overnight, and gently press the berries to extract all the juice.

Measure the juice, and allow 450g / 1lb preserving sugar per 600ml / 1 pint juice, putting both juice and sugar into a large, clean saucepan. Over heat, stir until the sugar has dissolved completely, and then boil fast for 15 minutes. Put a saucer into the fridge to chill. Draw the pan off the heat, drip some of the hot liquid onto the chilled saucer, leave for 5 minutes then gently push the surface of the dribble with your fingertip. If the surface wrinkles slightly, the desired set has been achieved. Pour into warmed, scrupulously clean jam jars, seal each with a disc of waxed paper, cool then seal each jar, label, and store on a shelf in a cold room.

NB: If the dribble does not wrinkle, then put the pan back on the heat and boil fast for a further 5 minutes before taking the pan off the heat to test again. Always take the pan off the heat while testing. The faster the boil, the sooner the set is reached, and the brighter the colour of your jelly – and also, the fresher its flavour. The longer this is boiled, as for any jelly or jam, the more the sugar caramelises and the darker the colour becomes.

Makes about 2 × 400g pots (warm a third pot just in case)

900g / 2lb rowan berries, stripped from their woody stalks

3 eating apples (e.g. Cox's), chopped – skin, core, the lot

450g / 1lb preserving or granulated sugar per 600ml / 1 pint of strained liquid

Pinhead Oatmeal, Lemon and Shallot Stuffing

Serves 6 (stuffs 2 pheasant)

50g / 2oz butter

1 onion, skinned and finely diced

2 sticks of celery, trimmed and peeled with a potato peeler to remove the stringy bits, then sliced very thinly

220g / 8oz pinhead oatmeal*

1 tsp salt, about 15 grinds black pepper

Rind of 1 lemon, finely grated

1 large egg, beaten

This stuffing is simple, extremely nutritious and, most importantly, it is packed with flavour. You can use it to stuff pheasant, partridge – especially French, or red-legged partridge, which in my opinion need all the help with flavour they can be given – and it can also be served baked in a buttered dish with roast grouse, instead of buttery fried-parsley breadcrumbs.

Melt the butter in a sauté pan and fry the onion and celery, stirring occasionally, for 5–7 minutes. Then add the pinhead oatmeal to the pan, stir well and cook for a further 5–7 minutes, stirring from time to time. Stir in the salt and black pepper, take the pan off the heat and cool the contents.

When cooled, mix in the lemon rind and the beaten egg, combining thoroughly. Divide between 2 pheasant (or 4 partridge), stuffing the mixture into the body cavity.

Alternatively, put the mixture into a buttered, fairly shallow ovenproof dish. Cut a further 50g / 2oz butter into small bits and dot them evenly over the surface. Bake in a moderate heat (180°C / 350°F / gas 4) for 40–45 minutes. The surface should be crisp.

* If you have difficulty sourcing pinhead oatmeal, try a health food shop.

Butter-baked 'Fried' Bread

Some game birds – e.g. pheasant, grouse and partridge – are delicious served on fried bread. But frying bread is a last-minute chore. My sister, Liv Milburn, taught me many decades ago how to bake 'fried' bread, which is every bit as good as frying, yet far more convenient. She coats her buttered bread in sesame seeds first, which adds an extra dimension to the flavour. And for those of us who eat in the same room in which we cook, it is one less cooking fragrance to dispel! This fried bread keeps warm satisfactorily. And you use very little butter when it is melted then brushed on the bread rather than being spread with a knife.

Melt the butter and stir in the salt.

Lay a sheet of baking parchment on a baking tray.

Brush both sides of each slice of bread with the melted butter, putting each onto the baking parchment when buttered. Bake in a hot oven (200°C / 400°F / gas 6) for 10 minutes – ALWAYS set the timer! Check that it is golden brown before turning each slice and baking for the same time on the other side. Keep the 'fried' bread slices warm until you are ready to serve, with sliced pheasant, or in the case of grouse or partridge, with a bird sitting on top of each slice.

Serves 6

6 slices baked white bread, about 1cm thick, crusts removed

50g / 2oz butter

1 tsp salt

Apple, Thyme, Shallot and Horseradish Sauce

Serves 6

3 banana shallots, skinned and neatly diced

2 tbsp olive or rapeseed oil

3 Bramley cooking apples, quartered, peeled, cored and chopped

Rind of 1 lemon, finely grated

1 sprig of thyme, the leaves stripped from the stalks (or ½ tsp dried thyme leaves)

2 tsp horseradish sauce

1 tsp salt, about 10 grinds black pepper

This is an excellent sauce for serving with roast wild duck, of any variety, and also with roast wild boar. It freezes very well, can be made up to two days in advance of eating, and it can be served either hot or cold. But only cooking apples must be used for this: they fall into a soft mush on cooking, whereas eating apples retain their chopped or sliced shapes. The flavour of Bramley cooking apples is superb as a background taste for the shallots, horseradish and thyme in this sauce.

Heat the oil in a saucepan and, over a moderate heat, fry the diced shallots for 5–7 minutes, stirring from time to time, so that they cook evenly. Then add the chopped apples to the contents of the pan, and stir in the lemon rind, thyme leaves, horseradish, salt and black pepper. Stir well, cover the pan with its lid and cook the contents gently, over a moderate heat, until the apples fall to a soft mush, about 15 minutes. Beat the contents of the saucepan with a wooden spoon, then tip the sauce into a serving dish. Cool, cover and store in the fridge or freeze until required.

Game Gravy

Game gravy should be thin, never thick. Be sure to save the fat from the roasting tin, scraped and poured off to add to the butter for the gravy. There won't be much to pour, but think of all the flavour that will come from the bacon that covered the birds, and from the butter put within the birds before roasting!

In a saucepan, combine the butter with the fat scraped from the roast game tin and stir in the flour. Cook for a couple of minutes on a moderate heat before stirring in the red wine or port. Cook this for a minute, stirring all the time, and then gradually add the stock, stirring until the gravy simmers gently. Stir in the gravy browning, redcurrant jelly and Worcestershire sauce. Serve the gravy very hot (you can store the hot gravy in a thermos jug if that is more convenient). Freeze any leftover gravy, to be used up in stews, casseroles or soup.

Serves 6

25g / 1oz butter

1 level tbsp flour

1 tsp salt, about 15 grinds black pepper

150ml / ¼ pint red wine or port

600ml / 1 pint good game stock (even better if this is reduced)

A dash of gravy browning – literally no more than a teaspoon

1 tsp redcurrant jelly

1 tbsp Worcestershire sauce

Green Peppercorn and Ginger Butter Sauce

Serves 6

2 tbsp granulated sugar

150ml / ¼ pint red wine vinegar

300ml / ½ pint game or vegetable stock

300ml / ½ pint port

5cm / 2" piece root ginger, peeled and finely diced

2 fat cloves garlic, peeled and finely diced

175g / 6oz butter, cut into bits

2 tsp green peppercorns, drained of their brine

This sauce enhances any roast venison, roast partridge, roast wild duck or wild boar. It is a real winner of a sauce. It can be made in advance but it should be reheated cautiously and never allowed to boil.

Put the sugar and vinegar into a saucepan over moderate heat and stir until the sugar has dissolved. Boil fast until the vinegar has almost evaporated – there should be a small puddle of vinegary caramel in the base of the saucepan. Pour in the stock and port – there will be a whoosh of steam, be warned – and add the diced ginger and garlic. Stir and simmer until the liquid has reduced by half. Add the butter, a bit at a time, and whisk it into the sauce, the pan off direct heat as you do so. Lastly, stir in the green peppercorns. Don't let the sauce simmer or boil once the butter is added. Serve hot.

Prune and Red Wine Sauce

This is very good with most roast game, including venison fillet, or wild boar, and with roast pheasant, partridge or any of the wild duck species. In fact, it is delicious with everything! I serve this sauce (and the following recipe – Madeira and Mushroom sauce) when I feel the need for a change from the traditional bread sauce, game chips and gravy accompaniments.

Melt the butter in a saucepan and fry the diced shallots over a moderate heat for about 5 minutes – the shallots should be soft and transparent, but not turning colour. Then stir in the flour and let this cook for a couple of minutes before gradually stirring in the red wine. Stir and cook until the sauce bubbles, then gradually stir in the stock.

Stir until the sauce simmers again, then stir in the redcurrant jelly, orange rind, salt and black pepper. Lastly, stir in the halved Agen prunes.

This sauce can be made a day in advance, then reheated to serve. It won't deteriorate at all, either in taste or in texture.

Serves 6

2 banana shallots, skinned and finely diced

50g / 2oz butter

1 rounded tbsp flour

300ml / ½ pint red wine (a fruity red, e.g. sangiovese or cabernet sauvignon)

450ml / ¾ pint stock (game, chicken or vegetable)

1 tsp redcurrant jelly

Rind of 1 orange, finely grated

1 tsp salt, about 15 grinds black pepper

9 Agen prunes, each cut in half (use scissors for this)

Madeira and Mushroom Sauce

450g / 1lb flat mushrooms, diced into thumbnail-size chunks

2 tbsp olive oil

1 tsp salt

2 banana shallots, skinned and finely diced

300ml / ½ pint Madeira

1 rounded tbsp flour mixed thoroughly with 50g / 2oz very soft butter

1 tsp salt, about 10 grinds black pepper

450ml / ¾ pint stock (game, chicken or vegetable)

This is another sauce which is so useful, and delicious, when the palate becomes a bit jaded by the traditional accompaniments to roast game!

Start by roasting the diced mushrooms, to give them a delicious flavour. Put the mushrooms on a roasting tin, add the olive oil and salt and, with your hands, mix the salt and oil thoroughly into the diced mushrooms. Spread them evenly over the base of the roasting tin and roast in a hot oven (200°C / 400°F / gas 6) for 30–35 minutes.

Meanwhile, put the shallots and Madeira into a saucepan. Bring to simmering point, and simmer gently for 12–15 minutes, the pan half covered with its lid. Add the stock to the contents of the pan and bring the liquid back to simmering. Cook for a further 5 minutes then mix some of the hot liquid into the butter and flour combination, mix well, then mix this into the hot liquid in the pan, stirring all the time. Cook until the sauce simmers. Stir in the salt and black pepper, and the roast mushrooms. Serve hot.

Watercress, Chicory and Pink Grapefruit Salad with Mustard and Walnut Vinaigrette

This salad makes a wonderful alternative to hot vegetables, to be served on a salad plate with any roast game bird – but not with venison or wild boar. The chopped fried walnuts in the slightly mustardy vinaigrette complement the flavours of the watercress and chicory, and the pink grapefruit is both palate-cleansing and delicious.

Heat the olive oil and fry the chopped walnuts with the salt and black pepper for about 5 minutes on a moderately high heat, stirring from time to time. Take the pan off the heat and cool the contents. When cooled, mix in the mustard and pink grapefruit juice.

Spoon and pour the dressing over the watercress, chicory and pink grapefruit segments in a serving bowl. Mix thoroughly.

Serves 6

75g / 3oz watercress, snipped with scissors to short lengths

2 heads chicory, sliced across into lengths about 1 cm thick

3 pink grapefruit, peel and pith removed with a sharp serrated knife, then slice the segments in towards the centre of each grapefruit, slicing between the white membranes to achieve pith-free segments (collect the juice as you slice the fruit, because it is good in the dressing)

For the dressing

5 tbsp olive oil

50g / 2oz chopped walnuts

1 tsp salt, about 10 grinds black pepper

1 tsp Dijon mustard

1 tsp salt, about 10 grinds black pepper

Up to 2 tbsp pink grapefruit juice

Shallot and Blackcurrant sauce

Serves 6

450g / 1 lb fresh or frozen blackcurrants

Sprig of thyme

3 banana shallots, skinned, halved and finely diced

2 tbsp olive oil

1 rounded tsp soft brown sugar

1 level tsp salt, about 15 grinds of black pepper

450mls / ¾ pint vegetable stock

As I write, blackcurrants are in season, but it is easy to buy frozen blackcurrants year-round. Spread on a tray, they thaw in ten minutes. This sauce is sharp but not sour. It is very good with all wild duck, but also with venison and wild boar. It is a convenient sauce in that it can be made in advance by 48 hours and stored in the fridge when cooled. It doesn't deteriorate at all when reheated to serve. But the blackcurrants must be gently simmered till tender with no sugar added to them – the sugar prevents the currant skins from tenderising. The pureed blackcurrants form the thickening for the sauce.

Put the blackcurrants and sprig of thyme into a saucepan and immerse in cold water. Over a fairly high heat, bring to a gentle simmer and continue to do so for 10–15 minutes, or until when you fish a currant out, its skin is tender. Take the pan off the heat and cool. Drain off the cooking liquid, discard the thyme and pulverise the cooked blackcurrants in a food processor, then sieve the resulting puree to get rid of the tiny seeds.

Heat the olive oil in a saucepan and over a moderate heat fry the finely diced shallots, stirring in the soft brown sugar, salt and black pepper. Cook for 8–10 minutes – till the shallots look transparent. Add the stock to the contents of the pan, and simmer gently. Then mix in the blackcurrant puree, stirring thoroughly. Simmer the sauce gently for 5 minutes before serving.

N.B. Sieving the pureed blackcurrants isn't an essential, but the tiny seeds remain in the puree if you choose not to sieve. Be warned!

PHEASANT

This chapter contains more recipes than any other chapter because pheasant is the most widely accessible of all types of game, both feathered and furred. Pheasant is just so versatile – it can be used in all recipes which call for chicken. Providing that the birds are hung, pheasant is a delicious meat, with great potential for combining with a wide variety of other tastes and textures.

The pheasant season starts on 1st October and continues until the last day in January. As the season progresses, pheasant becomes less and less expensive, and it is a form of protein which we should all make the very most of during its season. But do ask, when you buy from your butcher or game dealer, to be sure that the pheasant has been hung. Hanging makes all the difference in the world, both to the flavour of the bird and to the texture. There is only one aspect of pheasant that can detract from its delicious eating, however it is cooked, and that is that pheasant is a dry meat. This potential dryness is why the birds are draped with streaky bacon before being roasted. But really pheasant is no more dry than chicken, so please don't let this put you off trying pheasant if you haven't eaten it before.

Please note that pheasant vary in size, and cocks (male) are bigger than hens (female).

Roast Pheasant

Traditional roast pheasant is so very good at the start of the pheasant season. But as the season wears on, then comes the desire to vary the methods of cooking and serving this bird. If you have a plentiful supply, roast more pheasant than is required, in order to make the leftovers into a pheasant fricassee which, believe me, is very worth making for another pheasant feast!

Serves 6

2 brace pheasant (4 birds), ideally 2 cocks and 2 hens

12 rashers top-quality dry-cured unsmoked streaky bacon, each rasher cut in half

50g / 2oz butter per bird

Put the birds onto a roasting tin, and put the butter into the cavity of each bird.

Cover each bird with the halved bacon rashers. Roast in a moderate heat (180°C / 350°F / gas 4) for 1¼ hours. I prefer to roast them at this moderate temperature rather than at a higher heat because I find that the meat remains more succulent.

Take the birds out of the oven – if you are in any doubt that they are cooked (ovens vary much more than you would suppose), stick a small knife in between the leg and breast; the juices should run clear. If the juices are at all pink-tinged, put the pheasant back in the oven for a further 10 minutes' roasting time.

When roasted, leave the pheasant in their roasting tin and cover with foil. Leave to stand for 10 minutes. Drain off the buttery bacon fat juices from the roasting tin, into a saucepan for making into the gravy, and reserve a couple of tablespoons of the fat in a small bowl for making into a fricassee tomorrow with the leftover pheasant meat.

Carve the breasts, and serve the roast pheasant, with some of the bacon if you wish, accompanied by bread sauce (see p.22), game chips (p.26) and gravy (p.31). I like to serve a green vegetable with roast pheasant, such as steamed Brussels sprouts tossed in seasoned butter, or stir-fried Savoy cabbage – or for something a little different, try the chicory and watercress salad on p.35.

Pheasant Fricassee

Serves 6

The fat from the roasting tin, plus 1 tbsp olive or rapeseed oil

2 onions, skinned and neatly diced

2 sticks celery, trimmed and peeled to remove the stringy bits, then sliced finely

2 carrots, trimmed and peeled, then neatly diced

4 rashers dry-cured back bacon, sliced into thin strips

1 rounded tsp medium curry powder

1 rounded tbsp flour

300ml / ½ pint full milk

600ml / 1 pint stock (preferably game stock but chicken will do)

75g / 3oz plump sultanas

1 tsp salt, about 20 grinds black pepper

500–675g / 1–1¼ lb leftover roast pheasant meat, cut from the carcases, any skin or sinews discarded, the pheasant cut into small, even-sized chunks

The word 'fricassee' can conjure up some awful dishes in the minds of some people. If you are one such person, then please banish all thoughts of white sauce containing chunks of dry pheasant, because a good pheasant fricassee is worth roasting the birds just to make it! Don't be put off by the tiny amount of curry powder; it is just a part of the whole taste of the dish. Serve with boiled basmati rice and a green vegetable or salad.

Melt the pheasant dripping from the roasting tin in a casserole or stew pan and add the olive or rapeseed oil. Over moderate heat, fry together the onions, celery and carrots, stirring from time to time, for 12–15 minutes. Halfway through, stir in the strips of bacon, and continue to fry until the carrots are tender.

Stir in the curry powder, let it cook for a minute, then stir in the flour, and let the flour cook amongst the contents of the pan for a couple of minutes before adding the milk, stirring continuously. When all the milk is incorporated, stir in the stock, add the sultanas, salt and black pepper and stir the contents of the pan until it reaches simmering point. Let it simmer gently for 2 minutes, then add the pheasant meat.

Stir well, bring the sauce back to a gentle simmer and cook for 10 minutes, simmering very gently. Serve with either rice or very well-beaten mashed potatoes, and a green vegetable: petit pois are very good with this fricassee, as are any of the brassicas.

Pheasant Breasts with Onion, Curry, Brandy and Cream

This is a recipe which has stood the test of time. It's a real winner, and it makes a simple but great dish for a party. Just a word of warning: pheasant breasts tend to shrink more than chicken breasts do when cooked, so if the breasts are from a hen pheasant, allow for more than just one per person. (That is why I recommend slicing the breast meat before cooking.) This is good served with crispy roast potatoes and, as ever, a green vegetable of your choice.

Melt the butter in a wide sauté pan or casserole, and fry the sliced onions over moderate heat (don't let the butter burn) until soft and transparent, about 5–7 minutes. Then add the sliced pheasant meat to the pan and stir occasionally for another 5–7 more minutes. Stir in the curry powder, then add the brandy. Raise the heat and let the brandy bubble, then pour in the cream, salt and black pepper and stir thoroughly through the pheasant and onions. Let the mixture simmer gently for 2–3 minutes. Just before serving, stir the finely chopped parsley through the contents of the pan.

NB: This will keep warm without spoiling for 20–30 minutes. After cooking, but before adding the chopped parsley, cover the pan with its lid and keep it warm at a low temperature.

Serves 6

1.3kg / 1½lb uncooked pheasant breasts, skin removed (they may be skinned already) and the meat sliced into strips about 1cm thick

75g / 3oz butter

2 onions, skinned and thinly sliced

2 level tsp medium curry powder

150ml / ¼ pint brandy

450ml / ¾ pint double cream (it must be double in order that the cream thickens as it simmers)

1 tsp salt, about 20 grinds black pepper

1 heaped tbsp finely chopped parsley

41

Pheasant au Vin

Serves 6

2 pheasant

1 rounded tbsp flour

4 tbsp olive or rapeseed oil

12 banana shallots, skinned and halved lengthways

9 rashers back bacon, unsmoked, fat trimmed off (easiest done using scissors) and each rasher sliced into strips

675g / 1½ lb small mushrooms, stalks cut level with the caps

2 fat cloves garlic, skinned and finely diced

1 tsp thyme leaves – either fresh, stripped from the woody stalks, or dried thyme

1 tsp salt, about 20 grinds black pepper

1 bottle light and fruity red wine

This has a better flavour than the more traditional Coq au Vin. Cooked this way, a brace of pheasant goes further than if the birds were roasted.

Heat the oil in a large casserole. Cut each bird in half, then sprinkle with the flour. Brown the floured pheasant halves on either side, and as they are browned, lift them on to a large, warm dish.

Add the shallots to the casserole and fry them, stirring from time to time, until they are soft and transparent, about 5 minutes. Scoop them into the dish with the pheasant halves, leaving as much of the oil in the pan as you can.

Add the bacon and mushrooms to the pan, turning up the heat. Cook, stirring, until the mushrooms are browned, about 5 minutes. Then reduce the heat, replace the pheasant and shallots in the pan, add the garlic, thyme, salt and black pepper, and pour in the red wine.

Bring the wine to simmering point. Cover the pan with its lid, and cook in a moderate oven (180°C / 350°F / gas 4) for an hour.

Take the casserole out of the oven and cool the contents. When cooled, but not cold, lift out the pheasant halves and strip the meat from the carcases. (This is so much easier done before the birds are cold.) Replace the cooked pheasant meat in amongst the contents of the casserole.

This can be made 24 hours in advance: simply store in the fridge or a cold larder. As with all casseroles, the flavour is so much better when made in advance, cooled and reheated. Reheat on top of the cooker until the liquid simmers, then cover with its lid and simmer very gently for 10–15 minutes before serving. I love well-beaten mashed potatoes with pheasant au vin – the mash soaks up all the delicious juices.

Pheasant Braised with Chestnuts and Orange

I love chestnuts, and I think they enhance any game dish. In this easy recipe, the flavours of the chestnuts, shallots and orange go so well with the pheasant. As with the pheasant au vin, I like to serve well-beaten creamy mashed potatoes with this, and either roast roots such as carrots and parsnips, or a green vegetable – perhaps broccoli or purple sprouting, or Brussels sprouts. Sprouts are particularly delicious with the chestnuts in this casserole.

Heat the oil in a large casserole and brown the pheasant on either side. As they brown, lift them on to a warm dish. Add the shallots to the casserole and cook them, stirring from time to time so that they fry evenly, for about 5 minutes until they are soft and transparent.

Add the chestnuts, mix well, then stir in the flour. Cook for a minute before gradually adding the stock, stirring all the time. When it simmers, add the orange rind, salt, black pepper and balsamic vinegar.

Replace the browned pheasant in the casserole, and bring the liquid back to simmering. Cover the casserole with its lid and cook for 1 hour in a moderate oven (180°C / 350°F / gas 4).

Remove the casserole from the oven and cool. When cool enough to handle without scorching your fingers, lift out the birds and cut the meat from the carcases, discarding all skin, sinews and bones. Put the pheasant meat back into the casserole and mix well. Cool completely, then leave in a fridge or cold larder overnight.

Before serving, reheat on top of the cooker until the sauce simmers gently, then cover the casserole with its lid and simmer the contents very gently for 10–15 minutes before serving.

Serves 6

2 pheasant

3 tbsp olive or rapeseed oil

12 banana shallots, skinned and halved lengthways

450g / 1lb chestnuts*

1 rounded tbsp flour

900ml / 1½ pints good game stock (chicken will do as a substitute)

Juice and pared rind of 1 large orange (avoid any bitter white pith)

1 tsp salt, about 20 grinds black pepper

1 tsp good-quality balsamic vinegar

* Vacuum-packed chestnuts are obtainable everywhere these days, and are so easy to use. I buy them in the Co-op in Broadford, Isle of Skye.

Pheasant, Leek and Prune Soup

Serves 6

For the stock

1 pheasant

1 onion, skinned and stuck with 6 cloves

1 sticks celery, washed and broken in half

The washed outer leaves of the 6 leeks to be used in the soup recipe below

1 tsp salt, 1 tsp black peppercorns, bashed with the end of a rolling pin in a deep bowl

Pared rind of half a lemon (avoid any bitter white pith)

For the soup

1 tbsp olive or rapeseed oil

1 onion, skinned and neatly chopped

3 medium potatoes (preferably Rooster variety), peeled and chopped

6 trimmed leeks, finely sliced

The cooked pheasant meat cut from the carcase, finely sliced

9 Agen or no-soak prunes, cut into 4 bits

The reduced pheasant stock

Salt and black pepper to taste

With just one pheasant, six people can enjoy this excellent soup as a hearty main course. It is delicious, nutritious and sustaining served with crusty bread.

Put the pheasant into a large saucepan and immerse in cold water. Add the onion, celery, leek trimmings, pared lemon rind, salt and bashed peppercorns. Over heat, bring the water to a gentle simmer. Cover the pan with its lid and cook the contents gently for 1½ hours. Stick a knife in between a leg and the breast of the bird to check that the juices run clear. If they are still pink-tinged, replace the lid and cook the pheasant for a further 10–15 minutes.

Cool the pheasant in the liquid in the pan. When cold, lift out the pheasant. Strain the stock into a measuring jug, discarding the contents of the sieve. Wash out the pan and pour the stock into it – there should be a good 2 litres. Over heat, bring the stock to simmer. Simmer until the stock has reduced by a third. The flavours will concentrate as the stock reduces.

Carefully cut the cooked pheasant meat from the carcase, discarding all sinews, skin and bones. Cut the meat into small dice.

For the soup

Heat the oil in a large saucepan and fry the onion for about 5 minutes until soft and transparent. Add the potatoes and leeks to the pan and cook for a further 5–7 minutes, stirring from time to time. Add the stock, and when it reaches simmering point, half-cover the pan and simmer the contents gently for 15 minutes. Tip about half the contents of the pan into a bowl and, using a hand-held pulveriser, whiz the soup till smooth. Replace the pureed soup into the pan with the rest of the soup. Add the chopped prunes and the diced pheasant meat. Stir well, taste, and add more salt and black pepper if you think it is required. Ladle into warmed soup plates and serve with crusty bread.

Stir-fried Pheasant with Sugarsnaps, Ginger, Garlic and Lime

This recipe is full of flavour, and takes little more than five minutes to cook. The preparation time is about the same, providing you have that most time-saving of all kitchen gadgets – a really sharp knife! This is good served with couscous, or with boiled basmati rice.

In a large sauté pan, heat the olive oil until very hot. Stir-fry the strips of pheasant breast until they are opaque and cooked through – about 3 minutes, providing the pan is sufficiently hot.

Lift the cooked strips of pheasant from the pan into a warm dish, and add the spring onions, sugarsnaps, garlic and ginger to the pan. Stir-fry over a high heat for a further 3–4 minutes, then replace the pheasant strips in amongst the contents of the pan and stir in the toasted sesame oil, soy sauce, grated lime rind and juice, and the chopped coriander. There will be no need for salt for most palates, as the soy sauce provides saltiness.

Stir thoroughly, cook for 2 more minutes, then serve.

Serves 6

900g / 2lb pheasant breast meat, sliced into 1cm strips

3 tbsp olive oil

12 spring onions, trimmed at both ends and sliced in half lengthways

450g / 1lb sugarsnaps, each sliced into 3 bits, on the diagonal

2 fat cloves garlic, skinned and very finely diced

A 4cm / 2" piece of root ginger, peeled and finely diced

Finely grated rind of 2 limes and their juice

1 tbsp toasted sesame seed oil

2 tbsp dark soy sauce

Handful of coriander, coarsely chopped

Pheasant Casserole with Apples, Ginger and Celery

Serves 6

2 pheasant

3 tbsp olive or rapeseed oil

2 onions, skinned and finely sliced

1 head celery, each stalk trimmed at both ends, peeled to remove the stringy bits, then sliced on the diagonal into 1cm lengths

3 Bramley apples, each quartered, peeled, cored and chopped

1 tsp salt, about 20 grinds black pepper

The flavours within this casserole are light and delicious. The Bramley apples thicken the juices as they cook, falling obligingly to a soft puree, and the calorie content is low – although that changes if eaten with creamy mashed potatoes! Serve with one of the many green vegetables which so complement pheasant – Brussels sprouts, cabbage (my favourite is Savoy), broccoli or purple sprouting.

Heat the oil in a large casserole and brown the birds all over. Remove them to a warm dish once browned.

Add the onion to the casserole and fry, stirring from time to time, for about 5 minutes. Then add the celery to the casserole and fry, stirring from time to time, for a further 5 minutes. Stir in the Bramley cooking apples, salt and black pepper. Replace the browned pheasant in the casserole, pushing them down amongst the vegetables and chopped apples. Cook for 5 minutes, then cover the casserole with its lid, and cook in a moderate oven (180°C / 350°F / gas 4) for 1 hour.

Test to check that the birds are cooked by sticking a sharp knife into the bit between a leg and the breast of one of the birds. The juices should run clear – if they are pink-tinged, replace the lid on the casserole and continue to cook for a further 10–15 minutes.

Cool the cooked casserole and its contents. When the birds are cool enough to handle without scorching your fingers, lift them out and cut off all the cooked meat, discarding all skin, sinews and bones. Replace the pheasant meat in amongst the contents of the casserole and, when cold, store in either a fridge or cold larder. This can be made 24 hours in advance. Reheat on top of the cooker until the contents simmer gently. Replace the lid and simmer very gently for 10–15 minutes before serving.

Pheasant and Ham Lasagne

Serves 6

This is so good, and such a convenient dish too, as it can be made 24 hours before eating and reheated before serving. It only needs a dressed mixed-leaf salad as an accompaniment. Buy the best baked or roast ham you can for the ham content. Use the pheasant carcase to make into stock.

Put the raw chunks of pheasant meat into a food processor with the ham and pulverise briefly, careful not to whiz to a paste. You just want to break up the meats and combine them.

In a sauté pan heat the olive oil and add the minced pheasant and ham. Brown the meat over a fairly high heat, stirring to be sure that it browns and cooks evenly. Scoop the browned meat out of the pan.

Add the diced onions and fry them for 5 minutes, stirring occasionally, until they are soft and transparent. Replace the browned pheasant and ham and add the stock. Simmer gently, the sauté pan half covered, for 15 minutes. Cool.

Meanwhile put the milk into a saucepan with the onion, celery, salt, nutmeg and crushed parsley stalks. Over a moderate heat scald the milk until a skin forms, then take the pan off the heat and leave to infuse as it cools. When cold, strain the milk into a jug.

Make the sauce by melting the butter, stirring in the flour; let this cook for a couple of minutes then gradually add the strained flavoured milk, stirring continuously until the thin sauce boils.

Spoon half of the pheasant and ham mixture into a wide, shallow ovenproof dish. Cover with sheets of pasta, then pour in some of the white sauce, covering the pasta. The sauce is so runny so that it is absorbed by the pasta as it cooks. Spoon the rest of the meaty mixture over, cover with more sheets of pasta, and finish with the rest of the white sauce. Scatter the grated parmesan evenly over the surface.

Bake in a moderate heat (180°C / 350°F / gas 4) for 40–45 minutes. The surface should be golden brown. Stick a knife in the middle to test that the pasta is cooked.

---

1 cock pheasant, the meat cut from the carcase, discarding all skin and putting the carcase into a pan ready for making into stock

450g / 1lb roast or baked ham, chopped

2 tbsp olive oil

2 onions, skinned and finely diced

1 large clove garlic, skinned and finely diced

½ tsp salt, about 20 grinds black pepper

600ml / 1 pint stock (preferably game but chicken or vegetable stock will do instead)

For the sauce

1.2l / 2 pints milk

½ raw onion

1 stick of celery, washed and broken in two

1 tsp salt, a good grating of nutmeg

Small handful of crushed parsley stalks

50g / 2oz butter

50g / 2oz flour

8–12 sheets lasagne (exactly how many depends on the size of your lasagne dish)

50g / 2oz grated parmesan cheese

Alternative Roast Pheasant: Pheasant with White Pudding Stuffing

Serves 6

3 pheasant

12–16 rashers top-quality unsmoked streaky bacon

525g / 18oz white pudding, the outer skin removed, the pudding divided evenly into 3 chunks

White pudding needs nothing added to it, but it is essential to buy from a butcher who you know makes an excellent white pudding. The famous 'Charlie Barley' – Charles Macleod, of Stornoway black pudding renown – also makes a delicious white pudding, but so, too, do numerous other excellent butchers. The richness of the white pudding counteracts the possible dryness of the pheasant meat – but still, streaky bacon is needed to drape over the birds before roasting.

Cover a roasting tin large enough for the 3 birds with a sheet of baking parchment – this makes washing up afterwards so much easier. Put the birds on the parchment and stuff each bird with a third of the white pudding.

On a board, stretch each bacon rasher with the blade of a knife, then cut each rasher in half and drape the halved rashers over each bird, covering the birds entirely.

Roast in a moderate oven (180°C / 350°F / gas 4) for 1¼ hours. To check that the birds are cooked, stick a sharp knife between the leg and breast: the juices should run clear. If they are still pink-tinged, put the roasting tin and the birds back in the oven to cook for a further 10 minutes.

Remove from the oven and cover the contents of the roasting tin with a piece of foil. Leave to stand for 10–15 minutes – the foil will keep the birds hot. Pour the fat from the roasting tin into a saucepan to make the gravy (see p.31).

Pheasant Breasts with Leeks, Lentils and Savoy Cabbage

This is both delicious and very low in calories. Just be aware that pheasant breasts shrink, inevitably, during their cooking, so allow more than one breast per person – any leftover can always be reheated the next day. Another plus-point of this dish is that everything – pheasant meat, vegetables and starch in the form of lentils – is cooked in one casserole or stew pan.

Heat the oil in a large casserole or stew pan and fry the onions, stirring from time to time, until they are soft and transparent, about 6–7 minutes. Scoop them out of the casserole into a warm dish, leaving behind as much of the oil as possible.

Brown the pheasant breasts on either side – you will need to do this in relays, depending on the size of the base of the casserole. As the pheasant breasts brown, remove them to the dish with the fried onions.

Add the sliced leeks to the casserole and cook, stirring occasionally, for 5–7 minutes, until softened.

Stir in the cooking apples, salt and black pepper, lentils and stock, then add the fried onions and browned pheasant breasts. Cook until the liquid reaches simmering point, then cover the casserole with its lid and cook in a moderate oven (180°C / 350°F / gas 4) for 1 hour.

Take the casserole out of the oven and cool the contents. Store in a cold place, either a larder or the fridge. This can be made up to this point 24 hours ahead.

Reheat the casserole over a moderately high heat. When the liquid has reached simmering point, add the Savoy cabbage, pushing the cabbage down amongst the pheasant breasts, lentils, leeks and onions. The apple will have fallen to mush. Replace the lid and simmer for about 15 minutes, until the cabbage is tender when stuck with a knife.

There really isn't any need to serve another vegetable with this pheasant dish, but if you are feeding hungry young men, a dish of well-mashed buttery potatoes is always a welcome addition.

Serves 6

9–10 pheasant breasts – either buy the breasts, or if you have whole birds, slice them from the carcases and make stock with the raw carcases

2–3 tbsp olive or rapeseed oil

2 onions, skinned and finely sliced

4 medium leeks, trimmed, outer leaves discarded and finely sliced

220g / 8oz Puy or Tuscan lentils

1 Bramley cooking apple, peeled, cored and chopped

600ml / 1 pint stock (use either pheasant, game, chicken or vegetable stock)

450g / 1lb Savoy cabbage, cut in half, the core cut away and each half cut into 4 fat slices

1 tsp salt, about 15 grinds black pepper

Pheasant Ragu for Pasta

Serves 6

2 pheasant, raw, the meat cut from the carcase – discard all skin, sinew and any gristle encountered – and cut into small bits

450g / 1lb top-quality pork sausages, skins removed

3 tbsp olive oil

2 onions, skinned and finely diced

2 sticks celery, trimmed at both ends, peeled with a potato peeler, to remove the stringy bits, then finely sliced

2 carrots, peeled and neatly diced

1 tsp salt, about 15–20 grinds black pepper

Sprig of fresh marjoram, tiny leaves stripped from woody stalks (or ½ tsp dried marjoram)

1 tbsp tomato puree

300ml / ½ pint stock (use pheasant, chicken or vegetable stock)

400g tin chopped tomatoes

150ml / ¼ pint red wine

This is a delicious and sustaining (by which I mean filling!) sauce which freezes well for a limited number of weeks – six at the most. I choose a fat ribbon pasta – pappardelle, ideally – to go with this sauce, as I would for the hare ragu (see p.90).

Heat the olive oil in a wide sauté pan and brown the skinned pork sausages, mashing them with the back of your wooden spoon, and browning thoroughly. Meanwhile, put the pheasant meat into a food processor and whiz briefly, to break it all up as if minced – but don't pulverise it completely.

When the sausagemeat is browned, scoop it into a large warmed dish and brown the minced pheasant over a high heat, stirring almost continuously as it browns. It will benefit from the fat from the pork sausagemeat in amongst the olive oil. When the pheasant mince is browned, scoop it into the dish with the browned sausagemeat.

You may need to add another tablespoon of olive oil to the sauté pan, then add the onions, celery and carrots, reduce the heat a bit, and cook, stirring occasionally, for 10–12 minutes. The onions should be soft and transparent-looking. Stir in the salt, black pepper, marjoram, tomato puree, stock, chopped tomatoes and red wine.

Cook and stir until the sauce reaches simmering point, then stir in the browned sausagemeat and minced pheasant. Stir until the mixture simmers once again. Cover the pan with its lid and cook, simmering very gently, for 1 hour. Take the lid off the pan and continue to cook, simmering gently, for a further 15–20 minutes.

Cook the pasta, stirring a tablespoon of olive oil through the cooked, drained pasta. Serve on warmed plates, with the pheasant ragu spooned on each serving of pasta.

Spiced Pheasant with Cumin and Apricots

When the word 'spiced' is used, many people assume a fiery concoction. But chilli is the only really hot spice! This recipe uses cumin for a gently spiced dish, the contents of which are so mutually compatible in flavour and texture. I like to serve it with boiled basmati rice and steamed sliced green beans containing chopped salted almonds.

In a large casserole heat the oil and brown the birds all over. As they brown, lift them onto a warm dish.

Reduce the heat slightly beneath the casserole and fry the shallots, stirring from time to time, for 6–7 minutes. Then stir in the garlic and the bashed cumin seeds. Stir well and cook for 2–3 minutes. Stir in the flour, mix well and cook for a further couple of minutes before gradually adding the stock, stirring continuously until all the stock is added and the sauce boils. Add the halved apricots.

Replace the browned birds in the casserole, bring the sauce around the pheasant to simmering point, cover the casserole with its lid and cook in a moderate oven (180°C / 350°F / gas 4) for 1 hour. Take the casserole from the oven and cool the contents. When the pheasant is cool enough to handle without scorching your fingers, lift them out of the casserole and onto a large board. Cut the cooked meat from the carcases, discarding all skin, bones and sinews, and replace the pieces of pheasant meat in amongst the rest of the contents of the casserole. Store in a cold place, a larder or fridge, overnight.

To reheat, take the casserole into room temperature half an hour before putting it on the cooker on a moderately high heat. Reheat until it reaches a gentle simmer, then replace the lid. Simmer the contents gently (I stress the word *gently* – no fast boiling) and heat for 15 minutes before serving.

Serves 6

2 pheasant

3–4 tbsp olive or rapeseed oil

9 shallots, skinned and halved lengthways

1 fat clove garlic, skinned and finely diced

2 tsp cumin seeds,* bashed in either a mortar with a pestle, or in a small deep bowl using the end of a rolling pin

1 rounded tbsp flour

750ml / 1¼ pints stock (preferably pheasant stock, but game or chicken stock will do)

220g / 8oz plump dried apricots, each cut in half

1 tbsp lemon juice

1 tsp salt, about 20 grinds black pepper

* Try not to buy ready ground cumin; the seeds have so much more flavour

Pheasant Meatballs with Herb and Garlic Sauce

Serves 6

For the meatballs

2 pheasants, the meat cut from the carcases and chopped into small bits (discard all skin, sinew and gristle, and make stock from the carcases)

450g / 1lb top-quality pork sausages, skins removed

2 tbsp olive or rapeseed oil, plus extra for frying the meatballs

3 shallots, skinned and finely diced

2 sticks celery, trimmed, peeled with a potato peeler to remove the stringy bits, and very finely sliced

1 tsp salt, about 15 grinds black pepper

2 tbsp chopped parsley

Finely grated rind of 1 lemon

4 tbsp flour sieved onto a plate

2 large eggs, beaten in a small bowl

This is such a convenient and delicious recipe. The pheasant meatballs can be made a day in advance of cooking, and the sauce is simplicity itself. It is good served with boiled basmati rice or well-beaten mashed potatoes, and with a green veg such as steamed purple sprouting or Brussels sprouts.

Heat the oil in a frying or sauté pan and, over a moderate heat, fry the shallots and celery, stirring, for 5–7 minutes, or until the celery is soft and the shallots are soft and transparent. Then cool the contents of the sauté pan.

Put the pheasant meat into a food processor and whiz briefly, to break it up as for mince, then add the skinned pork sausages to the processor and whiz again, to combine the minced pheasant with the sausagemeat. Scrape the contents of the processor into a bowl and add the cold fried shallots and celery, salt, black pepper, chopped parsley and finely grated lemon rind.

Put a sheet of baking parchment onto a large plastic tray or baking sheet.

Scoop out spoonfuls of the pheasant mixture and roll between your hands into small, even-sized balls, a bit larger than a walnut. Allow 4–5 meatballs per person. Roll each in flour, then dip into beaten egg, then roll again into the flour. Put each pheasant meatball onto the parchment-lined tray. When all the mixture is made into meatballs, loosely cover them with clingfilm and keep the tray in a cool place, larder or fridge.

To cook, heat 2–3 tablespoons of olive or rapeseed oil in a wide sauté pan. When hot, put the pheasant meatballs into the pan and leave for one minute before turning them over to brown on their other side. Allow to cook for a further minute, then roll the meatballs over and fry so that they are browned all over, about 3–4 minutes. Lift them from the pan into a warmed dish lined with a couple of thicknesses of kitchen paper to absorb excess oil. Serve with the parsley and garlic sauce.

For the sauce:

Blanch the garlic by putting the whole cloves into a small saucepan. Immerse them in cold water, and put the pan on to heat. Bring the water to the boil, drain it away and replace it with cold water. Repeat this blanching process three times in total. Snip the ends of the garlic cloves and their flesh should pop out from the skins. Crush the blanched garlic – it has a much milder flavour when blanched. Heat the crème fraiche in a saucepan, adding the crushed blanched garlic cloves, salt and black pepper, mix well and, just before serving, stir in the finely chopped parsley. Serve the sauce, a small amount spooned over each serving of pheasant meatballs.

For the sauce

2 tubs of crème fraiche, either full-fat or half-fat*

2 fat cloves garlic, in their skins

2 tbsp finely chopped parsley

I tsp salt, about 15 grinds black pepper

* Choose whichever is dictated by the rest of the menu – i.e. whether the main course is to be followed by a creamy pudding or preceded by a creamy or cheese first course. In either case, I use half-fat crème fraiche, but the sauce is best made with the full-fat version – and it's so comforting, knowing that such creaminess can now be described as beneficial to our health! (Let's forget the calories . . .)

Pheasant Herb Schnitzels with Creamy Chive, Grated Apple and Horseradish Sauce

Serves 6

9 pheasant breasts

2 large eggs, beaten well with a fork, on a large plate

220g / 8oz baked white bread, crusts cut off before weighing

50g / 2oz parsley, tough stalks removed

25g / 1oz chervil

25g / 1oz chives, snipped finely with scissors

1 tsp salt, about 15 grinds black pepper

50g / 2oz butter and 2 tbsp olive oil

In this recipe the pheasant breasts are bashed – I use a rolling pin – to a thin escalope. These are then dipped into beaten egg then a breadcrumb and herb (parsley, chives and chervil) mixture before being fried in a butter and oil combination. They are delicious, and I like to serve them with a simple sauce of crème fraiche, snipped chives, horseradish and grated eating apples. All that is required is a steamed green veg to go with it – broccoli, purple sprouting or Brussels sprouts – and creamy mashed potatoes.

Start by making the herb crumbs. Put the crustless bread, torn into chunks, into a food processor with the parsley and chervil (NOT the chives) and whiz together until fine crumbs. Add the salt, black pepper and the snipped chives and whiz briefly, just to combine everything. Tip the contents of the processor onto a large plate.

Prepare the pheasant breasts by putting them, individually, between two pieces of baking parchment. Bash with a rolling pin until the breasts are as thin as possible. As they are transformed from pheasant breasts to escalopes, lift them from between the parchment and dip each on both sides into the beaten eggs, then press each side into the herby crumbs. As they are coated, put the pheasant schnitzels onto a large plastic tray. Cover loosely with clingfilm and store in a cold place – larder or fridge – until half an hour before you are ready to cook them.

Take the escalopes up to room temperature half an hour before frying. Heat the oil and melt the butter together in a large sauté pan and, when very hot, fry each schnitzel on either side until the crust is golden brown – about 2 minutes on each side. Lift them onto a warm dish lined with a couple of thicknesses of absorbent kitchen paper and cover loosely with foil, to keep in the heat. Serve with the following sauce.

Creamy Horseradish and Grated Apple Sauce

Put the ingredients for the sauce in a bowl and mix thoroughly, lemon juice included. Serve in a bowl, to accompany the herby pheasant schnitzels.

For the creamy horseradish and grated apple sauce

Serves 6

2 tubs crème fraiche (full fat or half fat)

3 tsp horseradish relish

2 good eating apples, washed, coarse-grated and mixed with 2 tbsp lemon juice

I tsp salt, about 10 grinds black pepper

I tbsp finely snipped chives

Pheasant and Roasted Mushroom Puffed Pie

Serves 6

For the filling

2 pheasant

2 onions, skinned and halved

2 sticks of celery, broken in half

Small bunch crushed parsley stalks

I tsp salt, 20 grinds black pepper

650g / 1¼lb flat mushrooms, cut into fat dice, stalks removed

8 rashers unsmoked air-cured back bacon, sliced into thin strips

2 tbsp olive oil

50g / 2oz butter

2 onions, skinned and finely diced

I tbsp flour

750ml / 1¼ pints reduced pheasant stock

I tbsp lemon juice

150ml / ¼ pint double cream

For the crust

I × 320g packet all-butter puff pastry

I large egg, beaten with a fork, for brushing the pie before baking

The secret to this dish is the roasting of the mushrooms with the bacon. The flavour is vastly better than if the mushrooms are fried, and an added plus-point to roasting them is that only a fraction of oil is required, whereas when mushrooms are fried they absorb oil like blotting paper. Buy only all-butter puff pastry, ready rolled out, as it tastes so much better than the non-butter varieties.

Two days before the pie is destined for the table, cook the pheasant by putting them into a casserole and immersing them in cold water. Add the vegetables, parsley stalks, salt and black pepper. On top of the cooker bring the water to a gentle simmer, cover the casserole with its lid and cook in a moderate oven (180°C / 350°F / gas 4) for 1 hour. Cool the contents of the casserole, lifting the birds out and onto a large board when they are cool enough to handle.

Cut all the meat from the birds, discarding the skin, sinews and gristle, and put the bones back into the pan containing the cooking liquid and veg. Put this pan back on to cook, and simmer very gently, the pan uncovered, until the liquid has reduced by two thirds. Strain, throwing away the contents of the sieve, and cool. When cold, skim off any fat from the surface of the concentrated pheasant stock, and measure the amount needed for the sauce for the pie. Any leftovers can be frozen.

Meanwhile, put the diced mushrooms and bacon strips onto a roasting tray and add the olive oil. With your hands, mix the oil into the mushrooms, spread the lot in an even layer and roast in a hot oven (200°C / 400°F / gas 6) for 35–40 minutes. (The mushrooms will shrink as they roast.) Take the pan out of the oven and cool.

Make the pheasant pie filling by melting the butter in a large casserole or saucepan and fry the finely diced onions, stirring occasionally, for 5–6 minutes or until they are soft and transparent. Stir in the flour and let it cook for a couple of minutes before gradually adding the stock, stirring continuously until the sauce simmers. Simmer gently for a minute then stir in the lemon juice and double cream – it must be double, because cream with a lesser fat content could curdle. Stir in the roasted mushrooms and bacon. Taste the sauce, and add salt and black pepper if you think it is needed. Add the pieces of cooked pheasant, tip the contents of the saucepan into an ovenproof dish and allow to cool.

Put an inverted egg cup in the centre of the pie. Brush around the edges of the dish with beaten egg, then lay the rolled-out puff pastry on the top making sure that the pastry is gently pressed down around the edges. Stick a knife into the surface of the pastry in half a dozen places – this allows steam to escape as the pastry bakes. Brush the entire surface with beaten egg.

Bake in a hot oven (200°C / 400°F / gas 6) for 15 minutes, then lower the heat to moderate (180°C / 350°F / gas 4) and continue to bake for a further 30–35 minutes. Check on the pie to make sure the pastry doesn't scorch: it should be well puffed and light golden brown.

This pie is very good with forcemeat balls served as an accompaniment, and any green vegetable of your choice.

Pheasant and Pistachio Terrine

Serves 6–8 as a first course, 6 as a main course.

For the marinade

300ml / ½ pint red wine

150ml / ¼ pint olive oil

2 banana shallots, skinned and finely diced

Pared rind of 1 orange and 1 lemon (use a potato peeler to do this, to avoid any bitter white pith)

1 tsp salt, about 25 grinds black pepper

3 bashed juniper berries

For the terrine

675g / 1½lb raw pheasant meat, diced to thumbnail size

450g / 1lb best pork sausages, skins removed

75g / 3oz shelled pistachios, unsalted

12 best quality unsmoked streaky bacon rashers

This is a versatile dish, which can equally be a first course, or a main course served with baked jacket potatoes and a dressed mixed leaf salad with a mustardy vinaigrette. It is so good to eat, but a word of warning: like the game terrine (p.13), it does not freeze at all successfully – it crumbles when sliced, having thawed. BUT it can be made and frozen uncooked. Be sure that it is completely thawed before cooking: allow 36 hours for it to thaw in a cool place, larder or fridge, and stick your finger down the middle of the raw terrine to check for any icy particles before cooking it.

Put the ingredients for the marinade into a saucepan and heat until the wine and olive oil reach simmering point. Simmer gently for 5 minutes, then take the pan off the heat and cool the contents completely. When cold, remove the strips of orange and lemon rind.

Put the diced pheasant meat and skinned pork sausagemeat into a large bowl and add the cold marinade. With your hand – which is the only way to mix thoroughly – combine the marinade with the pheasant meat and the pork sausagemeat. Leave for a couple of hours. Then mix in the shelled pistachios thoroughly, so that they are evenly distributed amongst the meats.

Prepare a terrine tin by lining a large, wide loaf tin with foil, gently easing it into each corner.

On a board, stretch each bacon rasher with the blade of a knife and put them, widthways, on the foil lining the terrine tin. Spoon in the pheasant mixture, and when it is all in, bang the terrine down three or four times on a work surface, to settle the contents. Flip the ends of the rashers over and then crimp the foil together.

Put the terrine into a roasting tin, and pour boiling water to come halfway up the side of the terrine. Cook in a moderate oven (180°C / 350°F / gas 4) for 2 hours. Take the roasting tin and its contents out of the oven, lift the terrine out and put it in a cool place with a weight on top (e.g. a couple of tins of tomatoes) to press down the cooked terrine as it cools.

When cold, lift off the weight and store the cooked terrine for up to 48 hours in the fridge. Unwrap the foil and turn the terrine out onto a serving plate and serve, thickly sliced.

Pheasant Breasts in Lemon and Brandy Sauce

Serves 6

9 pheasant breasts

75g / 3oz butter and 1 tbsp olive oil

1 rounded tbsp flour, sieved on a plate with 1 tsp salt and 15 grinds black pepper

300ml / ½ pint good stock (preferably pheasant but chicken will do instead)

150ml / ¼ pint brandy

150ml / ¼ pint lemon juice (NB: during marmalade orange season, Seville orange juice can be used instead)

2 tbsp mixed finely chopped parsley and snipped chives – to garnish

This is a light and convenient dish which can be prepared the day before it is to be eaten. It is best served with buttery mashed potatoes and a green vegetable such as steamed Brussels sprouts, fried Savoy cabbage, or roast chopped courgettes. Allow more pheasant breasts than the number of people, because they do shrink during cooking.

Prepare the pheasant breasts by putting them between sheets of baking parchment and bashing each with the end of a rolling pin, to flatten them out.

Dip each pheasant escalope into the seasoned flour, on both sides.

Melt the butter and heat the oil together in a wide sauté pan over a high heat – which is why you need the olive oil, to prevent the butter from burning. Cook the pheasant escalopes on each side for 2 minutes.

As they brown, lift the escalopes into a wide, shallow ovenproof dish. When they are all browned and cooked through, put foil over them in their ovenproof dish, to keep them hot.

Add the brandy to the pan, swirl it around, then stir in the stock and the lemon juice, let the liquid in the pan bubble for a minute before pouring the sauce over the cooked pheasant escalopes. Keep the dish warm until you are ready to serve.

Puff Pastry with Parma Ham, Garlic Mushrooms, Mozzarella and Leftover Pheasant

This is a delicious way to eke out a small amount of leftover trimmings from roast pheasant carcases. It is a wonderful first course, and it can be taken on picnics – remember to slice before transporting. The thickly seeded top of the puff pastry roll gives an added dimension to the taste and texture of this delicious dish, inspired by something I ate while in Rome one January.

To roast the mushrooms and garlic together on a roasting tin, mix the olive oil and black pepper through the diced mushrooms, spread them evenly on the tin and put in a hot oven (200°C / 400°F / gas 6) for 35–40 minutes. Cool.

To assemble, line a baking tray with a sheet of baking parchment. Unroll the puff pastry onto the parchment. Cover it with the slices of Parma ham, and spoon the cooled roast garlic mushrooms over the middle of the ham. Put the bits of leftover pheasant on the mushrooms, and a line of torn mozzarella down the centre.

Brush the edges of the pastry with beaten egg and fold the long edges over. Fold and tuck the short edges in and under to form a secure parcel. Carefully turn over the pastry roll, so that the seam is underneath – this is easier than it sounds when you are actually doing it! With a sharp knife, cut lines in the pastry on the diagonal, 1 cm apart, in both directions, giving a diamond-pane effect. Brush the entire surface with beaten egg and scatter the salt-seasoned seeds over the entire roll.

Bake in a moderate heat (180°C / 350°F / gas 4) for 35–40 minutes. Take it out of the oven and leave to stand for 20–25 minutes, uncovered, before slicing to serve.

NB: If the mozzarella seeps liquid during baking, tip the liquid down the sink and don't worry. Check the roll for this during baking, about halfway through the cooking time.

Serves 6

1 × 320g packet all-butter puff pastry, ready rolled

8 slices Parma ham

450g / 1lb mushrooms, diced to thumbnail size

2 fat cloves garlic, skinned and diced

2 tbsp olive oil

15 grinds black pepper

2 balls of top-quality buffalo mozzarella, drained of its preserving liquid and torn into even-sized chunks

Leftover slivers of cooked pheasant meat no bigger than 2cm / 1in. in size – smaller, if possible. (The amount doesn't matter, as it is bound to vary according to how much you have left over.)

1 large egg, beaten with a fork in a small bowl

2 tbsp mixed seeds (e.g. sunflower, pumpkin and sesame seeds)

1 tsp salt, mixed into the seeds

Pheasant and Pink Peppercorn Risotto

Serves 6

Pheasant stock

1–2 pheasant carcases, from the leftover roast birds

2 litres of cold water

3 onions, skinned and halved

4 sticks of celery, broken in half

1 stick of lemongrass, bashed with a rolling pin to yield more flavour

A handful of parsley stalks, bashed, as for the lemongrass, for the same reason

20 grinds of black pepper

1 teaspoon salt

For the risotto

2 onions, each skinned, halved and finely diced

3 tablespoons olive oil

500g / 1¼lb risotto rice

150ml / ¼ pint dry white wine – my choice is for a sauvignon blanc or a pinot grigio

1.5l / 3 pints pheasant stock

1 tsp salt, about 15 grinds of black pepper

2 tsp pink peppercorns, drained of their brine

50g / 2oz butter, cut into small bits

Leftover roast pheasant meat, cut into as evenly sized bits as possible

1 rounded tbsp finely chopped parsley

This is an excellent recipe in which to use leftover roast pheasant. It is one of those recipes which can accommodate a small amount of leftover pheasant and pad it out to give a delicious main course. The pink peppercorns in the recipe give that small pop of flavour in each mouthful which is so satisfying – but buy the pink peppercorns in brine, as opposed to the dried ones. The pheasant stock for this dish is all-important, and the finely chopped parsley stirred through the risotto just before serving adds to the visual appeal as well as to the flavour.

Put the stock into a large saucepan over heat until the water reaches simmering point. Cover the pan ingredients and simmer gently for 2 hours. Then remove the lid and simmer for a further 30 mins, to reduce the liquid and therefore concentrate the flavours within. Cool the stock, then strain into a large measure jug or two, and discard the contents of the sieve.

Heat the olive oil in a wide saute pan and fry the diced onions, stirring occasionally, over a moderate heat for about 5 minutes. Then stir in the rice, stirring for 2–3 minutes so that each grain is coated with oil. Then stir in the white wine and let this evaporate before stirring some of the pheasant stock into the contents of the sauté pan. Cook over a gentle to moderate heat – stir occasionally. Add more stock and the pink peppercorns, and continue adding the stock as each addition is absorbed by the risotto rice. Leave a small amount of stock in the jug. Stir the bits of butter through the risotto, and the salt and pepper, and 10 minutes before serving stir the pieces of pheasant meat through the risotto. Stir in the remaining stock and the finely chopped parsley, and serve – the texture of the risotto should be almost sloppy, but absolutely not stiff. This is very good with a vinaigrette-dressed mixed leaf salad.

GROUSE

Surely the most Scottish of all birds is the grouse –
Lagopus lagopus scotica is its Latin name. Grouse, whose
season starts on 12 August and closes on 10 December, has
a mystique all its own as a species of game bird. Young
grouse are a true delicacy. They should be hung for 4–5
days – but not, mercifully, for so long that they turn green
and fall from their hooks. This is how previous generations
liked to eat their grouse, and it is memories of grouse hung
to this extent which make mainland Europeans shiver with
dread at the very thought of being given roast grouse, and
no wonder!

Roast grouse is traditionally eaten on fried bread,
accompanied by bread sauce and game chips, and buttery
fried breadcrumbs. Recipes for these are to be found in the
Game Accompaniments chapter. A thin gravy, and a
watercress salad on a salad plate, are the only other things
required, but I prefer steamed sliced green beans when I
eat roast grouse. Roast grouse is a treat. Cold roast grouse
is a delicacy. Old grouse is delicious too, just never to be
roasted – it is far too tough. Old grouse has an excellent
flavour and is useful in dishes requiring lengthy braising or
cooking.

Black game are a part of the grouse family. The
distinctive curly tail feathers of the black game cocks (the
female of the species are called grey hens) were worn in
the bonnets of the pipers of the former Argyll and
Sutherland Highlanders Regiment and also the pipers of
the Gordon Highlanders. Now, these tail feathers are worn
by the soldiers of the Royal Regiment of Scotland.

All recipes for grouse can be used for black game as well.

Roast Grouse

Whether you allow one bird per person or just half a bird per person depends entirely on whether you are giving your guests a first course and a pudding as well. If the roast grouse is to be the main course of a three-course dinner or lunch, then half a bird is perfect. If, on the other hand, the main course is to be followed by a light, fruity pud, then a whole bird is required. Recipes for the accompanying bread sauce, buttery parsley breadcrumbs, fried bread and gravy are all to be found in the Game Accompaniments chapter.

Put the grouse onto a roasting tin with a knob of butter inside each bird. Drape 4 halves of bacon rasher over each bird. Roast in a hot oven (200°C / 400°F / gas 6) for 10 minutes, from room temperature. Then reduce the heat to moderate (180°C / 350°F / gas 4) and roast for a further 40 minutes. Take the birds out of the oven, tip the fat from the roasting tin into a saucepan for the gravy, and let the birds sit, loosely covered with foil to keep them warm, for 10–15 minutes. Serve each bird on a piece of butter-baked bread – so much better than actually frying the bread – and serve the bread sauce, parsley crumbs and gravy separately. If you like – and I do – have a dish of apple and rowan jelly (see p.27) on hand to eat with the roast grouse.

Serves 6

6 young grouse

12 rashers top-quality air-cured unsmoked streaky bacon, each rasher cut in half

6 x 25g / 1oz knobs butter

15 grinds black pepper

Braised Old Grouse with Shallots and Damsons

Serves 6

6 old grouse

3 tbsp olive or rapeseed oil

12 banana shallots, skinned and halved lengthways

2 fat cloves garlic, skinned and diced

2 tsp Demerara sugar

450g / 1lb damsons

600ml / 1 pint game stock, reduced if possible (chicken stock will do instead, but it is second best)

1 tsp salt, about 20 grinds black pepper

1/4 tsp ground cinnamon – absolutely no more

50g / 2oz very soft butter

2 level tsp flour

Damsons are my favourite fruit for a number of reasons. They taste delicious, they make wonderful jams and jellies, they form the best puds, and they are delicious cooked with old grouse. It is well worth the small amount of time taken to pre-cook the damsons so that you can get rid of their stones before putting the stoneless fruit into the casserole with the old grouse. This dish is best eaten with buttery mashed potatoes and steamed Brussels sprouts – the slight sweetness of the sprouts is so good with the taste of the grouse and damsons.

Heat the oil in a sauté or casserole pan and brown each grouse on each side, removing them as they brown to a large, warmed dish. Add the shallots and garlic to the pan and fry over moderate heat for 5–6 minutes. Towards the end of this time stir in the Demerara sugar and cook for a further 2 minutes.

Meanwhile, put the damsons into a saucepan with the stock. Cover the pan with a lid, and bring the stock to simmering point. Cook gently for 5 minutes, take the pan off the heat and cool. When cool enough to handle the damsons, lift out each one and remove the stone, putting each damson into the sauté pan or casserole with the fried shallots, garlic and Demerara sugar. Only this way can you be absolutely sure to have removed every single damson stone.

Replace the browned grouse in the casserole and, through a sieve, pour the damson stock into the casserole (the sieve will catch any damson stone that might possibly have escaped). Season with salt, black pepper and the tiny amount of cinnamon and bring the liquid to a simmer.

Cover the pan and cook in a low to moderate heat (150°C / 300°F / gas 3) for 2½ hours. Take the casserole from the oven and cool. When the cooked grouse are cool enough to handle, lift each out and onto a board and cut the meat from the carcases, placing the grouse meat in amongst the damsons and shallots in the casserole. Leave overnight in a cold place (larder or fridge).

To reheat and complete the dish, mix together the soft butter and flour in a small bowl or mug. Take the casserole into room temperature for half an hour before putting it onto a moderately high heat. Reheat until the liquid gently simmers, then mix a small amount of hot liquid into the butter/flour mixture, mix well, then stir this into the contents of the casserole, mixing it in as best you can, and stir until the liquid simmers again. Cook, with lid on, the contents very gently simmering, for 15–20 minutes. Serve.

Young Grouse with Agen Prunes and Parma Ham

Serves 6

6 young grouse breasts

12 slices Parma ham

12 Agen prunes

Black pepper (no need for salt, as the Parma ham contributes enough)

25g / 1oz butter

1 tbsp olive oil

1 tsp flour

300ml / ½ pint Madeira

300ml / ½ pint game stock (chicken stock is a second-best substitute)

For those who have a glut of grouse (such luck!) this is a delicious way to cook the breasts of young birds. The flavours of the prunes, Parma ham and grouse go together very well. The breasts can be prepared hours in advance of cooking them, and they are very good accompanied by cauliflower in a creamy sauce, and with roast or sautéed potatoes. You will notice that I allow one breast per person. That is because the Parma ham and prunes make them fairly filling, and I feel two is just too much!

Lay out 6 slices of Parma ham. Cut each Agen prune in half and put one on each slice of ham. Put a grouse breast on top of the prune, and grind black pepper, about 5 grinds, onto the grouse.

Put a second prune on each grouse breast and cover each with a second slice of Parma ham. Fold each into a neat parcel, tucking the ham from underneath and on top neatly in towards the meat.

At this point you can leave the prepared grouse breast parcels on a plate or board, loosely covered with clingfilm, in a cool place, a larder or fridge, for a few hours or overnight. Take them into room temperature for half an hour before cooking.

In a wide sauté pan melt the butter and heat the olive oil until hot. Put the grouse parcels into the pan and cook, on a moderately high heat, for 10 minutes, turning the parcels over and over so that they cook evenly. Lift the parcels from the pan onto a warmed serving dish and bake in a hot oven (200°C / 400°F / gas 6) for 10 minutes.

Meanwhile, stir the teaspoon of flour into the juices in the pan, and cook for a minute before adding the Madeira and stock; stir with a flat whisk until this simmers, then take the grouse in its ovenproof dish out of the oven, and pour the juices from the sauté pan over the parcels in the dish. Loosely cover with foil and keep the dish and its contents warm in a low-temperature oven until you are ready to serve, but not for much longer than 20 minutes.

Young Grouse Breasts Butter-fried with Walnuts and Orange

Here is another idea for young grouse breasts. It's a quick but delicious dish, which benefits from being accompanied by roast carrots and parsnips, and steamed leeks in a creamy sauce. The taste of the fried walnuts with the grouse is sublime.

Melt the butter in a wide sauté pan and add the grouse breasts, walnuts, salt and black pepper. Over a moderate heat – beware burning the butter – cook the grouse breasts in the butter, with the walnuts, turning over the breasts from time to time, and stirring the walnuts around when you do so. Cook for 20–25 minutes. Then stir the finely grated orange rind and the orange juice into the buttery pan juices, and dish up the grouse breasts on a warmed serving plate or ashet, with the fried orange walnuts spooned over the breasts. Loosely cover the plate and its contents with foil, to keep in the heat, until you are ready to serve.

Serves 6

12 young grouse breasts

75g / 3oz butter

120g / 4oz walnut halves (fresh if possible – if not, check the sell-by date on any packet of walnuts you buy)

1 tsp salt, about 20 grinds black pepper

Finely grated rind of 1 large orange and its juice

Old Grouse Braised with Celery, Apples and Puy Lentils

Serves 6

6 old grouse

3 tbsp olive or rapeseed oil

2 onions, skinned and finely sliced

1 head celery, trimmed and peeled with a potato peeler to remove the stringy bits, then each stalk sliced on the diagonal into lengths about 4cm / 2" long

4 good eating apples (e.g. Cox's), peeled, cored and quartered, then slice each quarter into 3 slices

220g / 8oz Puy or Tuscan lentils

600ml / 1 pint unsweetened apple juice

1 tsp salt, about 20 grinds black pepper

This is an excellent dish, full of flavour, but also packed with nutrition and low in calories – an all-round winner. It also benefits from everything – protein (grouse), vegetables (celery) and starch (lentils) – being cooked in one pot. There is no need for any other accompaniments, but a steamed green vegetable, such as Savoy cabbage, does just round off all the flavours and textures.

Heat the oil in a large casserole and brown each bird on all sides. As they brown, lift them onto a warm dish. Lower the heat slightly beneath the casserole and fry the onions, stirring from time to time, for 5–6 minutes, until they are soft and transparent. Add the celery and chopped apples to the onions, mix well and season with salt and black pepper. Cook for a further 4–5 minutes, stirring occasionally. Then stir in the lentils.

Replace the grouse, pushing them down amongst the contents of the casserole. Lastly, pour in the unsweetened apple juice. Bring the liquid to simmering point before covering the pan with its lid, and cook in a low to moderate oven (150°C / 300°F / gas 3) for 2 hours. Take the casserole out of the oven, cool, lift the grouse out and put them onto a board. Cut the meat from the carcases, and replace the cooked grouse meat in amongst the contents of the casserole. Cool completely and store overnight in a cold place – a larder or a fridge.

To reheat, take the casserole into room temperature for half an hour, then reheat on top of the cooker, until the liquid simmers. Replace the lid, and simmer the contents very gently for 15–20 minutes before serving.

Grouse and Madeira Soup

This is a thin, elegant soup, and it is also a good way to use up old birds. The flavour of Madeira is so good with that of the grouse. This is also a way of cooking additional old birds which can then be used for making into grouse paté (see recipe on p.72).

For the stock

Heat the oil in a large pan and brown each bird on both sides with the bacon rashers. Then add the rest of the ingredients to the browned birds in the pan. Pour in the water and put the pan on a fairly high heat, bring the water to a simmer, cover the pan and cook, gently simmering, for 2½–3 hours. Cool the contents of the pan completely, then lift out the birds and cut the meat from each. Put the meat into a bowl and cover with clingfilm. Skim any fat from the cold stock, then pour the contents of the pan through a sieve into a measuring jug. Discard the contents of the sieve.

For the soup

Melt the butter and fry the onions, carrots, potato and bacon over a moderately high heat, stirring fairly frequently, for 7–10 minutes. Add the black pepper and the grouse stock. Bring to a gentle simmer, uncovered, for 15–20 minutes. Then add the Madeira, bring back to simmering for 2 more minutes. Take the pan off the heat and blitz the contents using a hand-held blender till very smooth. Taste, and add salt and more black pepper if you think it is needed. Reheat gently and, just before serving, stir the finely chopped parsley through the soup.

Serves 6

For the stock

6 old grouse

2 tbsp olive or rapeseed oil

2 rashers best-quality unsmoked back bacon

2 onions, skinned and halved, each half stuck with 2 cloves

2 carrots, preferably organic

2 sticks celery, broken in half

Small bunch parsley stalks, crushed to release their flavour

1 tsp salt, about 25 grinds black pepper

3 bashed juniper berries

3 litres of cold water

For the soup

50g / 2oz butter

2 onions, skinned and chopped

2 carrots, trimmed, peeled and chopped

1 potato, peeled and chopped

2 rashers best-quality back bacon, unsmoked, fat cut off and the bacon chopped

20 grinds black pepper

900ml / 1½ pints grouse stock

300ml / ½ pint Madeira

2 tbsp finely chopped parsley

Grouse Pâté

Serves 6

The flesh from 3 old, cooked grouse
(see the recipe for grouse and
Madeira soup on p.71)

3 slices roast or boiled ham, fat
included

2 tbsp olive oil

2 banana shallots, skinned and
chopped

2 tsp redcurrant jelly

2 tbsp Worcestershire sauce

About 20 grinds black pepper

175g / 6oz butter, melted very slowly
on a very, very low heat (e.g. the back
of an aga or on a radiator)

I like to put this pâté into small pots and seal them with clarified butter. It is best served with Melba toast.

Heat the olive oil and fry the shallots over moderate heat for 7–10 minutes. Stir in the redcurrant jelly and Worcestershire sauce, and mix in the black pepper.

Put the grouse meat and ham into a food processor and whiz, adding the shallots and their liquid from the pan. Whiz it all to a smooth texture, then divide the pâté between 6 small pots or ramekins.

Carefully pour the clarified butter from the pan, leaving behind the white curdy part in the bottom of the pan. Leave the butter to set on each pot of pâté, then cover each with clingfilm and store in a cold place, larder or fridge, for up to 48 hours before serving.

PARTRIDGE

Partridge make me feel hypocritical. To me, they are the most enchanting birds. Yet English or grey-legged partridge are my favourite of all game to eat. There is a vast difference between English (grey-legged) and the more common French, or red-legged partridge. The flavour of the English variety, I believe, is superior to that of the French counterpart. Perhaps for diplomatic reasons I should from now on refer to them by the colour of their legs rather than by their nationality!

Grey-legged partridge are wild birds, whereas to a large extent, red-legged partridge are bought and reared, like pheasant. When served traditionally, whichever their leg colour, partridge are roasted, draped with streaky bacon, and accompanied by bread sauce, game chips and buttery fried parsley crumbs. I think that of all game birds, roast partridge is best accompanied by a watercress salad on a side plate, but green beans or broccoli (either purple sprouting or plain) are also very good.

The recipes in this chapter, apart from straight roast, are really for the red-legged variety of partridge, because I think they need culinary assistance with their flavour, and the red-legged are the variety to be found for sale up and down the land in most supermarkets. One bird per person is the right amount for a lunch or dinner consisting of one main course with a light pud. But if the partridge is to be a main course for a three-course meal, then half a bird per person could be enough. You will be the judge!

Roast Partridge (Grey-legged)

The recipes for the accompanying bread sauce, game chips, fried parsley breadcrumbs and gravy are all to be found in the Game Accompaniments chapter.

Put the birds onto a roasting tin with a knob of butter inside each bird. Cover each bird with 4 halves of streaky bacon and grind black pepper over each one.

Roast in a hot oven (200°C / 400°F / gas 6) for 45 minutes, then take the roasting tin out of the oven and loosely cover the birds with foil, to keep in their heat, and leave them to rest for 10–15 minutes. Carefully drain the fat from the roasting tin into a saucepan to make the gravy (see p.31).

Serves 6

6 grey-legged partridge

12 rashers top-quality air-dried streaky bacon, unsmoked, each rasher cut in half widthways

6 x 25g / 1oz butter

Black pepper

Roast Partridge (Red-legged) with Jerusalem Artichoke Timbales and White Wine and Shallot Sauce

Serves 6

6 red-legged partridge

12 rashers top-quality unsmoked streaky bacon, each rasher cut in half widthways

6 x 25g / 1oz knobs butter

Black pepper

For the timbales

450g / 1lb Jerusalem artichokes, weighed when peeled, cut into even-sized chunks and cooked in 600ml / 1 pint chicken stock until soft (keep the stock for the sauce)

4 large eggs

300ml / ½ pint single cream

1 tsp salt, about 15 grinds black pepper, a grating of nutmeg

This is such a convenient recipe. The mixture for the Jerusalem artichoke timbales can be made 24 hours in advance of cooking, providing that it is given a good stir before being poured into the buttered ramekins to bake. Both the roast partridge and the timbales need to stand for 15 minutes before being served, and the white wine and shallot sauce can be made in its entirety 24 hours in advance, only needing to be reheated to serve, spooned over each timbale.

Put the partridge into a roasting tin with a knob of butter inside each bird. Cover each bird with 4 halves of bacon rasher. Grind black pepper over the birds. Roast in a hot oven (200°C / 400°F / gas 6) for 45 minutes, then take the roasting tin out of the oven and cover loosely with foil, to keep the birds hot. Let them rest for 15 minutes before serving.

To make the mixture for the timbales, cook the artichokes in the stock with the lid on over a moderate heat until the artichokes are very soft when squished against the side of the pan with the back of a wooden spoon. Take the pan off the heat and cool the contents. Lift the cooled artichokes into a food processor, add the salt and black pepper, and whiz until smooth. Keep the stock for the sauce.

Beat the eggs together with the cream, and mix in the pureed artichokes thoroughly. Cover and leave in either a larder or fridge until half an hour before cooking, when the container must be taken into room temperature.

Thoroughly butter 6 ramekins and divide the artichoke mixture evenly between them. Put the ramekins into a roasting tin and pour boiling water into the tin to come halfway up the sides of the ramekins. Bake in a moderate oven (180°C / 350°F / gas 4) for 25–30 minutes or until they feel quite firm to touch. Take the roasting tin from the oven and leave to stand, the tin and its contents loosely covered with foil to keep in the heat, for 15 minutes. To serve, turn a knife around the inside of each ramekin and invert onto warmed plates, shaking the ramekin to dislodge its timbale.

For the sauce, put the diced shallots, white wine and artichoke stock into a saucepan over moderate heat. Bring the liquid to simmering point and simmer gently, the pan covered, for 10–15 minutes, or until the shallots are soft.

Thoroughly mix together the flour, butter and salt. Mix some of the liquid into the flour and butter combination, then mix this into the contents of the pan, stirring until the sauce simmers. Stir in the black pepper and cover the surface of the sauce with a disc of parchment if you make it in advance of serving. Remove the parchment to reheat and, just before serving, stir the finely chopped parsley through the hot sauce.

For the white wine and shallot sauce

4 banana shallots, skinned and finely diced

300ml / ½ pint dry white wine (my preference is sauvignon blanc)

600ml / 1 pint stock (use the stock flavoured with the Jerusalem artichokes during their cooking)

50g / 2oz soft butter

2 tsp flour

1 tsp salt

15 grinds black pepper

1 tbsp finely chopped parsley – to be added at the last minute before serving

Roast Partridge (Red-legged) with Watercress and Pea Sauce

Serves 6

6 partridge

12 rashers top-quality unsmoked streaky bacon, each rasher cut in half widthways

6 x 25g / 1oz knobs butter

Black pepper

For the sauce

3 banana shallots, each skinned and finely diced

50g / 2oz butter

600ml / 1 pint stock (either game or chicken is fine)

120g / 4oz petit pois, thawed from frozen

75g / 3oz watercress

1 tbsp lemon juice

1 tsp salt, about 15 grinds black pepper, a grating of nutmeg

This delicious sauce goes very well with the flavour of the partridge. It is a vivid green colour, and looks so attractive. I like to serve well-beaten mashed potatoes with the partridge and the sauce, along with roasted carrots and leeks.

Put the partridge into a roasting tin with a knob of butter inside each bird. Cover each bird with 4 halves of bacon rasher. Grind black pepper over the birds. Roast in a hot oven (200°C / 400°F / gas 6) for 45 minutes, then take the roasting tin out of the oven and cover loosely with foil, to keep the birds hot. Let them rest for 15 minutes before serving.

To make the sauce, melt the butter in a saucepan and, over a moderate heat, fry the diced shallots for 5–6 minutes.

Put the thawed peas into a food processor with half the stock and whiz until smooth. Add this to the fried shallots in the saucepan. Simmer gently for 2–3 minutes.

Meanwhile, put the watercress into the processor with the remainder of the stock and whiz until smooth. Stir this into the contents of the saucepan. Simmer gently for 1 minute, adding the lemon juice, salt, black pepper and nutmeg.

Serve the sauce separately for your guests to help themselves.

Roast Partridge with Roast Shallots and Beetroot

In this recipe the birds are roasted in amongst the shallots and chunks of beetroot, but you will see that the birds still have their drape of streaky bacon, as in every recipe for roasting partridge. The dash of balsamic mixed in with the roasted shallots and beetroot doesn't taste remotely of vinegar – please do not worry that it might – but it does just cut through the sweetness of the roasted beetroot. A good buttery mash is delicious with this, and a green veg such as steamed Savoy cabbage or purple sprouting broccoli rounds off this main course perfectly.

Put the shallots and chunks of beetroot into a roasting tin. Add the oil, salt, black pepper and balsamic and, with your hands, mix all together thoroughly. Roast in a hot oven (200°C / 400°F / gas 6) for 20 minutes. Take the roasting tin out of the oven and mix the contents thoroughly, using a large spoon.

Put the birds on top of the vegetables, and put a piece of butter inside each bird. Drape each bird with 4 halved bacon rashers and grind black pepper over each bird. Put the roasting tin back into the oven and roast for 45 minutes.

Take the roasting tin out of the oven, and loosely cover the contents with foil. Leave to stand for 15 minutes before serving.

Serves 6

6 partridge

6 x 25g / 1oz knobs butter

12 rashers top-quality unsmoked streaky bacon, each rasher cut in half

6 banana shallots, skinned and halved lengthways

900g / 2lb beetroot, weighed before peeling, peeled and cut into chunks approx. 2cm in size

3 tbsp olive or rapeseed oil

1 tsp salt, about 20 grinds black pepper

1 tablespoon balsamic vinegar

Braised Partridge with Wild Mushrooms and Thyme

Serves 6

6 partridge

6 medium onions, skinned and finely sliced

450g / 1lb wild mushrooms (a combination of several types or just one type, e.g. chanterelle), sliced

4 tbsp olive oil

A sprig of thyme, the tiny leaves stripped from the woody stalks (or ½ tsp dried thyme)

1 tsp salt, about 20 grinds black pepper

600ml / 1 pint stock (either game or chicken stock will do)

2 tbsp lemon juice

300ml / ½ pint double cream

If you live in a place where you can pick wild mushrooms, then I urge you to go out and pick your own, but if you are at all unsure about what to pick, arm yourself with Roger Phillips' book, *Mushrooms*, which has the clearest illustrations and descriptions of what is and isn't poisonous. Better to be safe in what you pick! At Kinloch we are so lucky to have woods around us full of chanterelles, some horns of plenty (in Italian these are unnervingly called Trumpets of Death – but they are delicious and perfectly safe!) and hedgehog mushrooms. We also abound in ceps, but they are my least favourite. And if you cannot find wild mushrooms, then just use cultivated mushrooms instead – but remember the flat ones have much more flavour than the smaller, closed-cap mushrooms. Crispy pieces of potato roasted in olive oil with garlic are good with this dish, along with any steamed green vegetable.

Heat three tablespoons of olive oil in a wide casserole and brown the birds on either side. As they brown, lift them onto a large, warm dish, then add the onions to the oil in the casserole and fry, over a moderately high heat, for 5–6 minutes, stirring from time to time so that they fry evenly. Scoop them out of the pan and put them in with the browned partridge. Add more oil to the casserole, raise the heat beneath the pan, and fry the sliced wild mushrooms, stirring, so that they fry for about 5 minutes. Reduce the heat a bit then replace the fried onions in the casserole and add the salt, black pepper and stock. Bubble for a minute, then stir in the lemon juice and the double cream. Simmer the sauce in the casserole for a couple of minutes, then replace the browned partridge in the casserole, cover with its lid, and cook in a moderate oven (180°C / 350°F / gas 4) for 1 hour.

Take the casserole out of the oven, and serve.

Seared Partridge Breasts with Blood Oranges and Watercress Salad

With two partridge breasts per person this makes a delicious main course, accompanied by baked jacket potatoes, or one partridge breast per person makes a perfect first course.

Arrange the snipped watercress on 6 plates, dividing it evenly. Sieve the flour onto a plate and combine thoroughly with the salt, black pepper and finely chopped parsley. Dip each partridge breast into the flour and parsley mixture, pressing down firmly on each side.

Heat the oil in a wide sauté pan over high heat. Brown the partridge breasts on both sides, allowing a minute's cooking each side, then lift them on to the watercress on each plate. Add the sliced spring onions to the olive oil in the pan and stir-fry them for a minute, then add the blood orange slices, and let them cook for a couple of minutes. Spoon them and the spring onions over each of the partridge breasts.

Serve, warm or cooled, at room temperature. The heat of the cooked partridge breasts will wilt the watercress slightly.

Serves 6

6 partridge, their breasts sliced from the carcases with a sharp knife

2 tbsp flour

1 tsp salt

20 grinds black pepper

1 tbsp finely chopped parsley

4 tbsp olive oil

6 spring onions, trimmed at each end and finely sliced

6 blood oranges, their skin sliced from the fruit using a sharp serrated knife, then each orange sliced into rounds, as thinly as possible, discarding any pips

120g / 4oz watercress, snipped with scissors to bite-sized pieces

Salmis of Partridge

Serves 6

6 partridge

3–4 tbsp olive oil

4 rashers top-quality unsmoked back bacon, fat snipped off, the bacon cut into ½cm strips

9 banana shallots, skinned and halved lengthways

450g / 1lb flat mushrooms, stalks removed, the mushrooms sliced about 1cm thick

A sprig of thyme, tiny leaves stripped from the stalks (or ½ tsp dried thyme)

300ml / ½ pint red wine

300ml / ½ pint good stock (preferably game stock but chicken will do instead)

1 tsp salt, about 20 grinds black pepper

This is a delicious combination of partridge, bacon, mushrooms, red wine and thyme. Towards the end of cooking, blanched thick slices of Savoy cabbage are added to the casserole. This dish is best served with buttery, well-beaten mashed potatoes.

In a large casserole, heat the olive oil and brown the birds all over, removing them to a warm dish when browned. Next, stir-fry the mushrooms over high heat, adding more oil if necessary, for 3–4 minutes, then scoop them into the dish with the browned partridge. Reduce the heat slightly beneath the casserole and add the bacon strips and halved shallots to the casserole. Fry, stirring from time to time, for 5–6 minutes.

Pour in the red wine and stock, add the salt, black pepper and thyme, and bring the liquid to simmering point. Replace the mushrooms and mix well. Lastly, add the browned partridge, pushing them down amongst the contents of the casserole. Bring the liquid back to simmer, cover the casserole, and cook in a moderate heat (180°C / 350°F / gas 4) for 1 hour.

Take the casserole out of the oven, and when the birds are cool enough to handle put them onto a large board and carefully cut the cooked meat from each carcase, discarding all skin and bones and sinews. Replace the cooked meat in amongst the contents of the casserole. Store in a cool place, a larder or the fridge.

Take the casserole into room temperature half an hour before reheating. Reheat on top of the cooker, until the liquid is just simmering, then cover and cook, simmering very, very gently, for 15 minutes before serving.

HARE

Oh dear. I love hares; there is something magical about seeing one in the wild. But I also love eating them and so, yet again, as with partridge, I feel a hypocrite. Brown hares are most commonly available, but recently we were given two mountain (or blue) hares, which were larger than I expected them to be, but I think that is because it was February and not August, and they were fully grown. Hare is truly delicious, a delicacy. Yet I find that the meat is like Marmite: people either love it or loathe it. Luckily, in our family we all love it. In Italy, particularly in Tuscany and Umbria, hare ragu features on all menus, eaten with wide ribbons of pasta, usually pappardelle. Hare soup is one of the most comforting of dishes, roast saddle of hare with a creamy sauce is wonderful, but my favourite hare dish of all is jugged hare, with forcemeat balls.

Jugged Hare

The sauce for this dish is made rich and velvety smooth when the hare blood can be incorporated. But if you buy frozen hare and have none of the blood, then add extra port – double the amount in the ingredients listed here. Once the blood is added, the sauce should not be allowed to reach even the gentlest simmer as it could well curdle – the expression 'blood curdling' does have some foundation in fact! If at all possible, collect the blood from the hare. Even if it is only 2–3 tablespoons, the blood will elevate this delectable dish to its ultimate potential, giving an unctuous richness to the sauce.

This dish is enhanced by being served with well-beaten mashed potatoes, and with either Brussels sprouts, broccoli, or purple sprouting. And don't forget the forcemeat balls, the recipe for which is on p.21.

Serves 6

1 hare, cut into joints

50g / 2oz butter

2 tbsp olive or rapeseed oil

2 onions, skinned and each stuck with 5–6 cloves

2 carrots

2 sticks of celery, chopped

1 fat clove garlic, skinned and chopped

Pared rind of 1 orange

Pared rind of 1 lemon

Small bunch of parsley stalks, bashed to release their flavour

Large sprig of thyme

3–4 bashed juniper berries

1 rounded tsp salt

About 25 grinds black pepper

In a wide casserole melt the butter and heat the oil together, and brown each piece of hare on all sides. Add the onions, carrots and celery to the casserole, and cook for a further 5 minutes. Then add the chopped garlic, orange and lemon rinds, parsley stalks, thyme, juniper, salt and black pepper. Cover the contents of the casserole with cold water and, over a high heat, bring the water to a simmer. Cover the casserole with its lid and, from simmering, cook in a low to moderate oven (150°C / 300°F / gas 3) for 3–3½ hours. The meat should be falling from the bones. Take the casserole from the oven and cool completely.

When cold, lift out the pieces of hare and carefully remove all the meat, discarding all bones. Put the hare meat into a bowl. Measure out 1.2 litres / 2 pints of the hare stock, straining through a sieve, to use for the sauce (keep the remainder for making into hare soup later).

For the sauce

1.2l / 2 pints stock, from cooking the hare

50g / 2oz soft butter

50g / 2oz flour

150ml / ¼ pint port

2 tsp redcurrant jelly

Salt, black pepper, to taste

As much hare blood as possible (OR, as stated in the introduction to this recipe, double the amount of port)

To complete the jugged hare, in a clean saucepan heat the stock for the sauce. When it is hot, stir in the redcurrant jelly until it dissolves. Mix the butter with the flour until it is a smooth paste. Then mix some of the hot stock into the butter and flour mixture, mixing well. Stir this into the hot stock in the saucepan, adding the port. Stir until the sauce simmers, then cook gently for two minutes.

If you have hare blood, mix some hot sauce into the blood, then stir this into the sauce in the pan, but take care not to let the sauce simmer again once the blood is added. The texture of the sauce alters with the addition of the blood, and it is truly delicious.

Put the hare meat into the sauce, and reheat gently. Taste, and add more salt and black pepper if you think it is needed. Serve with a dish of hot forcemeat balls (see recipe on p.21) to accompany the jugged hare.

Roast Stuffed Saddle of Hare with Shallot Sauce

There isn't much meat on a saddle of hare, but it is the most delicate part of the beast. When stuffed, it forms a delicious main course. The flavours which most complement that of hare include onions, mushrooms, dried fruit (with prunes and apricots leading the list) and fresh fruit such as apples and pears —and citrus, too. Nuts, and especially chestnuts, are very good with hare. In the stuffing for this recipe, you will find pork sausagemeat, which reduces the risk of the hare meat being dry after roasting. For the same reason, streaky bacon drapes the saddle during roasting. The word 'stuffing' is something of a misnomer because in fact the 'stuffing' is put beneath the saddle as it roasts, rather than being encased by the hare meat.

To make the stuffing, heat the oil and fry the onions over moderately high heat, stirring occasionally, for 5–6 minutes until completely soft and transparent. Cool. Tip the cold fried onions into a bowl, and add the salt, black pepper and finely grated orange rind, plus the pork sausagemeat and the chestnuts. With your hands, thoroughly combine these ingredients.

Lay a sheet of baking parchment onto a roasting tin, and put the saddles onto this.

Shape the stuffing mixture into two even-sized amounts and form them beneath each saddle. Drape the bacon rashers over the saddles, cutting them if necessary, but covering each saddle with bacon.

Roast in a hot oven (200°C / 400°F / gas 6) for 45–50 minutes. Take the roasting tin out of the oven, and tip the juices from the tin into a saucepan to make the sauce. Loosely cover the contents of the roasting tin with foil, to keep them hot.

Serves 6

2 saddles of hare, on the bone (the bone helps prevent shrinkage during cooking, and following roasting, the meat is easily cut form the bone before being sliced to serve)

12 rashers top-quality unsmoked streaky bacon

For the stuffing

2 onions, skinned and finely diced

2 tbsp olive or rapeseed oil

1 tsp salt, about 15 grinds black pepper

Finely grated rind of 1 orange

450g / 1lb best pork sausages, skins removed

12 chestnuts (easiest bought in vacuum-sealed packs)

For the shallot sauce

Juices from the hare roasting tin

50g / 2oz butter

4 banana shallots, skinned and finely diced

50g / 2oz flour

600ml / 1 pint game stock (or hare stock if you have some, made from the rest of the hare)

150ml / ¼ pint port

1 tsp salt, about 15 grinds black pepper

1 tsp redcurrant jelly

150ml / ¼ pint double cream

To serve, lift the saddles onto a large board, slice the meat in one long strip from the bones, and slice fairly thickly. Put the sliced hare meat onto a warmed serving plate and spoon or slice the stuffing beside the hare meat.

Melt the butter in the saucepan with the juices from the roast hare and its stuffing, and fry the shallots, stirring occasionally, for 5–6 minutes. Then stir in the flour, cook for a couple of minutes before gradually adding the stock, stirring all the time, and the port. Stir until the sauce simmers, and add the salt, black pepper and redcurrant jelly. Stir in the double cream, and simmer gently. Serve with the sliced roast saddle of hare and its stuffing.

Hare Soup

When you have cooked the meat for jugged hare (see p.85) and have surplus stock, or, when you have a joint of hare, perhaps a leg or a bit of the skirt to be made into stock, it is well worth making into this delectable and sustaining soup. The old-fashioned way to serve hare soup was to accompany it with a dish of plain boiled potatoes – shaken dry, once drained, in their pan over heat – and they must be a floury potato: Rooster, Golden Wonder or Kerr's Pink are all exemplary varieties. People would then help themselves to a potato and put it into their bowl of hare soup.

Heat the oil and melt the butter in a large saucepan, then fry the liver for a couple of minutes, stirring. Scoop the liver out of the pan and put into a warm dish. Put the chopped onions in the pan and fry for about 5 minutes, stirring from time to time. Add the strips of bacon and cook, with the onions, for a further 3–4 minutes. Then add the chopped carrots and celery, and the strip of orange rind, and cook for a further 5 minutes, stirring occasionally.

Add the garlic and potatoes, and the stock, redcurrant jelly, salt and black pepper. Bring the stock to simmering point and cook, gently simmering, for 20–25 minutes, the pan uncovered.

With the back of a wooden spoon squish a bit of carrot against the side of the pan to be sure that it is cooked. Stir in the port, return the liver to the pan and whiz, with a hand-held blender, until very smooth. Taste, and add more salt and pepper if you think it is needed. Reheat before serving.

Serves 6

2 onions, skinned and chopped

2 carrots, peeled, trimmed and chopped

A strip of orange rind (pared using a potato peeler, to avoid any bitter white pith)

2 sticks celery, trimmed, peeled with a potato peeler to remove the stringy bits, then chopped

I fat clove garlic, skinned and chopped

2 potatoes, peeled and chopped

2 tbsp olive or rapeseed oil

50g / 2oz butter

I rasher unsmoked back bacon, fat cut off, and the bacon sliced into strips

220g / 8oz lamb's liver, trimmed of all membranes and cut into small chunks

I tsp redcurrant jelly

I tsp salt, about 15 grinds black pepper

1.2l / 2 pints hare stock

150ml / ¼ pint port

Hare Ragu for Pasta

Serves 6

2 hind legs of hare

3–4 tbsp olive oil

2 onions, skinned and finely diced

3 carrots, peeled, trimmed and finely diced

3 sticks celery, trimmed, peeled with a potato peeler to remove the stringy bits, then finely sliced

1–2 fat cloves garlic, skinned and finely diced

2 rashers unsmoked back bacon, fat removed, the bacon finely diced

1 level tbsp flour

1 rounded tbsp tomato puree

300ml / ½ pint hare stock (have another 300ml / ½ pint ready in case it is needed before reheating the sauce)

300ml / ½ pint red wine

1 tsp redcurrant jelly

1 tsp salt, about 20 grinds black pepper

This sauce is thick, hearty and so delicious. The hare meat is cooked until virtually shredded, and the vegetables have almost melted into the hare meat. It is a very good sauce for pasta.

Heat the olive oil in a pan and brown the hare legs on either side. When browned, lift them onto a warm plate. Add the onions, carrots and celery to the pan and stir well. Fry over a moderately high heat, stirring from time to time, for 8–10 minutes. Add the bacon and garlic to the pan, cook for a couple of minutes, then stir in the flour and cook for a further minute. Stir in the stock, tomato puree, red wine, redcurrant jelly, salt and black pepper.

Replace the hare legs in the pan, cover with a lid, and cook in a low oven (100°C / 250°F / gas 2) for 3–3½ hours. Take the pan out of the oven and cool the contents completely. Then, when cooled, remove the meat from the hare joints, taking care to discard all bones. Mix the hare meat into the rest of the sauce in the saucepan. If you think it is needed, stir in another 300ml / ½ pint hare stock.

Reheat and serve by placing a generous spoonful on top of each serving of cooked and drained pasta.

Hare and Chestnut Oat Crumble

This is one of those invaluable recipes in which the protein – the hare meat – and some starch – the chestnut oat crumble – is cooked in one dish. All that is needed alongside is a vegetable, and my choice is for a leafy green such as braised kale or broccoli, either purple sprouting or plain, whichever is available. The crumble mixture can be made up to 48 hours in advance if that is more convenient for you, and the whole pie can be assembled 24 hours in advance, needing only to be baked before eating.

Start by cooking the hare. Heat the oil in a large casserole and brown the hare all over. As it browns, lift it onto a warm dish. Add the clove-stuck onion to the casserole along with the sliced onions, and cook them, stirring occasionally, for 5–7 minutes until soft and transparent.

Stir in the flour and cook for a minute before gradually adding the cold water, stirring until the sauce simmers. Add the sliced apples, salt and black pepper, and bring the liquid back to simmer. Replace the browned hare joints in the casserole, let the liquid reach simmering again before covering the casserole and cooking in a moderate oven (180°C / 350°F / gas 4) for 1 hour 30 minutes. The meat should come easily away from the bones when ready.

Take the casserole out of the oven and cool. Remove the clove-stuck onion, then lift out the hare joints and remove the meat from the bones, replacing the meat in the casserole. Put this mixture into an ovenproof dish.

Serves 6

For the hare meat

2 hind legs of hare plus the skirt – the body, not the saddle

I onion, skinned and stuck with 5 cloves

3 tbsp olive or rapeseed oil

2 onions, skinned and thinly sliced

I rounded tbsp flour

3 good eating apples, peeled, cored and sliced

900ml / 1½ pints cold water

I tsp salt, about 20 grinds black pepper

For the chestnut and oatmeal crumble

50g / 2oz butter

1 onion, skinned and neatly diced

220g / 8oz porridge oats

12 chestnuts, halved (it's easiest to buy these vacuum packed)

1 tsp salt, about 15 grinds black pepper

Meanwhile, make the crumble by melting the butter in a wide sauté or saucepan. Fry the diced onion for 4–5 minutes, until soft, then add the halved chestnuts to the butter in the pan along with the salt and black pepper. Fry together for a couple of minutes, then add the porridge oats, mixing thoroughly. Cook, stirring from time to time, for 5 minutes then take the pan off the heat and cool the contents.

Cover the surface of the hare mixture with the crumble, distributing it evenly.

Keep the pie, covered with clingfilm, in a cold larder or fridge until half an hour before reheating. Take the pie into room temperature for half an hour before cooking in a moderate oven (180°C / 350°F / gas 4) until the hare sauce bubbles gently around the sides and the crumble is golden brown – about 45–50 minutes.

Hare Marinated and Casseroled with Blood Oranges and Shallots

The marinade for this dish also becomes part of the cooking ingredients. Blood oranges have a longer season than you might suppose, from mid January through to mid April, and their flavour is sharp yet distinctively sweet. The taste is very compatible with that of the hare, and the sweetness of the shallots just rounds off the flavours within this dish. I like to serve it with well-beaten mashed potatoes and a green vegetable such as Savoy cabbage or Brussels sprouts.

Serves 6

For the marinade

1 hare, cut into joints

1 onion, skinned and diced neatly

4 tbsp olive oil

Juice of 6 blood oranges

300ml / ½ pint red wine

About 30 grinds black pepper

For the marinade

Heat the oil and fry the diced onion for 4–5 minutes, then take the pan off the heat and mix with the blood orange juice and the black pepper in a wide dish – the blood orange juice will cool down the onions and oil immediately.

Put the hare joints into the dish and rub each joint with the marinade. Leave the hare to marinate for 12–24 hours, turning the joints over about three times during the marinating.

To cook the hare

To cook the hare, melt the butter and heat the oil in a wide casserole. Lift the hare joints from the marinade, pat each joint dry and brown in the butter, removing the hare joints to a large, warm plate as they brown.

Fry the halved shallots for 5–6 minutes, turning them over so that they cook all over. Then stir in the flour, salt and black pepper, cooking for a couple of minutes before adding the reserved marinade and the stock, stirring continuously until the liquid simmers. Replace the browned hare joints in the casserole, bring the liquid back to a simmer, cover and cook in a low to moderate oven (150°C / 300°F / gas 3)

To cook the hare

50g / 2oz butter

2 tbsp olive oil

12 banana shallots, skinned and halved lengthways

1 rounded tbsp flour

1 tsp salt, about 15 grinds black pepper

The reserved marinade from the hare

600ml / 1 pint stock (either hare, chicken or vegetable stock)

for 2½ hours. Take the casserole from the oven, cool, then lift out the joints and remove the cooked hare meat from the bones, replacing it in amongst the shallots in the casserole. Cover the casserole and store in a cold place, a larder or the fridge, for 24–36 hours.

To serve, take the casserole into room temperature half an hour before reheating. Reheat on top of the cooker until the liquid simmers, then replace the lid and heat in a moderate oven (180°C / 350°F / gas 4) for 30–35 minutes from simmering point.

This is very good accompanied by forcemeat balls (see recipe on p.21).

Hare Pudding

This sounds stodgy and very old-fashioned. Well, I suppose it is old-fashioned but it's far from stodgy, and it is utterly delicious. The suet crust is light if you use vegetarian suet, which has a lower fat content than beef suet. The hare meat is cut from the carcase and packed into the pastry with a red wine and redcurrant jelly stock. The lengthy steaming time allows all the delicious flavours from the hare meat to infuse the fragrant suet crust. Have a jug of hot stock and red wine to hand when you serve the pudding, to pour into the opened pudding in case it looks a bit dry.

Serves 6

For the suet crust

1 onion, skinned and very finely diced

1 tbsp olive oil

675g / 12oz self-raising flour, sieved

175g / 6oz suet, preferably vegetarian

1 tsp salt, about 10 grinds black pepper

Finely grated rind of 1 orange

Enough cold water to bind the ingredients

Start by making the sauce. Put the stock, wine, redcurrant jelly, salt and pepper together in a saucepan and heat until the jelly has melted. Simmer very gently. Cool before pouring into the hare pudding before cooking.

To make the suet pastry, heat the olive oil and fry the finely diced onion over a moderate heat for about 5 minutes, stirring once or twice to be sure of even cooking. Take the pan off the heat and cool.

Mix together the cooled fried diced onion, sieved flour, suet, salt and black pepper and finely grated orange rind, mixing in just enough cold water to bind the ingredients thoroughly. Turn onto a lightly floured work surface and knead briefly. Then break off a third and set on one side for the lid, rolling out the remainder to line a boilable plastic pudding bowl (about 1.8 litres / 3 pints capacity). The pastry won't come right up to the top, but it is so much better to cook this in a bigger bowl. Line with the rolled-out pastry and roll out the remainder to fit the lid.

For the filling

The meat cut from the hind legs and saddle of a hare, diced small, mixed with 2 onions, skinned and finely diced, plus 1 tsp salt and 20 grinds black pepper

1.2 litres / 2 pints hot game or hare stock

300ml / ½ pint red wine

2 tsp redcurrant jelly

1 tsp salt, 15 grinds black pepper

Pack the hare meat and diced onions into the lined pudding bowl. Pour in the cooled stock/red wine mixture, reserving some to serve alongside the pudding once cooked. Cover with the suet pastry lid and crimp together the edges. Put a disc of baking parchment on top of the suet pastry lid, snap the lid on the pudding bowl, and steam in a large saucepan containing simmering water to halfway up the sides of the bowl, the pan covered with its lid. Set a timer and regularly check the level of the water in the pan, taking the greatest care not to let it dry out. Steam for 5–6 hours, if you intend to cook the pudding in advance of eating – and the flavour is much better if you do cook this in advance. But if you want to serve it after its first cooking, then steam it for 6–7 hours.

Store the cooked hare pudding in either a larder or the fridge, and take it into room temperature an hour before re-steaming prior to serving. Steam for 1½–2 hours, taking care not to let the pan boil dry. When you serve the pudding, pour in some of the hot stock and red wine mixture.

WILD BOAR

I have been eating wild boar meat when in Italy since I was a child, and since Alexandra, our eldest daughter, married her Austrian/German husband Philipp, we've often eaten it when visiting them. These days, wild boar is increasingly available throughout the United Kingdom.

For those who aren't familiar with wild boar, just imagine venison crossed with pork, and you are almost there! The flavour is delicious, and the meat can be cooked in a variety of ways, depending on the cut. But as with all game, whether furred or feathered, the secret to both the flavour and the tenderness of the wild boar meat is in the hanging, which is essential. And for how many days? Well, that is entirely weather-dependent, but a minimum of five days if the weather is hot, and a maximum of 21 if the weather is very cold and frosty.

Wild boar meat is enhanced by fruit – especially apples and citrus in the form of oranges and occasionally lemons – and dried fruit, whether prunes, raisins or dried apricots. All members of the onion family are delicious cooked with wild boar, as are spices, in particular horseradish and paprika.

In Italy and Germany salami is made using wild boar, and very good it is too, but I have never felt inclined to make salami of any type at home! But roast wild boar, oh yes – whether a loin or a saddle – and braised, or made into a goulash, or casseroled . . . All these ways of cooking this delicious meat are very familiar to me and to our family and friends who have feasted on the results.

Wild Boar braised with Onions, Prunes and Balsamic

I use meat cut from the leg for this dish. This benefits from being cooked, cooled and reheated before eating. The flavours intensify so much better than if it is eaten after just being cooked. A buttery, well-beaten mash is my potato dish of choice with this, along with roast root vegetables, either just one type or a mixture, such as carrots, shallots and beetroot.

Put the meat into a large polythene bag with the flour and salt and shake the bag hard, to coat each chunk of meat with seasoned flour. Heat the oil in a large casserole and brown the floured meat, a small amount at a time, over a high heat. Brown the meat on all sides, and as it browns, use a slotted spoon to lift the browned meat into a warm dish. When all the meat is browned, reduce the heat slightly beneath the casserole and fry the onions, stirring and scraping the bits from the base of the casserole as you do, for 5–7 minutes until soft and transparent. Then stir in the garlic, stock and red wine, stirring and scraping the base of the dish, until the liquid simmers.

Replace the browned meat in the casserole, add the balsamic vinegar and the halved prunes, then bring the liquid back to simmering, cover the casserole and cook in a low to moderate oven (150°C / 300°F / gas 3) for 2 hours. Take the casserole out of the oven and cool. Store for up to 36 hours in either a cold larder or the fridge.

Take the casserole into room temperature half an hour before reheating to serve. Reheat on top of your cooker, until the sauce simmers, then cover the casserole and continue the reheating at a simmer, in a moderate oven (180°C / 350°F / gas 4) for 30–35 minutes.

Serves 6

900g / 2lb trimmed wild boar meat (weighed after trimming), cut into chunks

2 rounded tbsp flour

1 tsp salt and about 25 grinds black pepper

4–5 tbsp olive or rapeseed oil

3 onions, skinned and finely sliced

1 fat clove garlic, skinned and diced

650ml / 1¼ pints stock (either game vegetable stock)

300ml / ½ pint red wine

1 tbsp good quality balsamic vinegar

12 soft prunes, each cut in half

Roast Loin of Wild Boar with Leeks and Jerusalem Artichokes in Milk, and with Horseradish Mash

Serves 6

Approx. 1.8kg / 4lb wild boar loin on the bone

1.2l / 2 pints whole milk

3 tbsp olive oil

6 medium leeks, trimmed and outer leaves removed, then sliced about 2cm thick

1 onion, skinned and finely sliced

450g / 1lb Jerusalem artichokes, peeled and cut into even-sized chunks

1 Bramley cooking apple, peeled and chopped

A piece of root ginger about 4cm / 2" long, chopped quite finely, skin and all

1 tsp salt, about 25 grinds black pepper

In this recipe the milk (and it must be whole milk and not skimmed) makes the meat very soft as it cooks. The milk curdles unbecomingly, but when it is liquidised with the leeks and artichokes to form the sauce, and eaten with the horseradish-flavoured mashed potatoes, it contributes a most delicious main course. The red cabbage recipe (see p.24) goes perfectly with this.

Put the wild boar loin into a large casserole or deep roasting tin and pour the milk around it.

In a sauté pan, heat the oil and fry the leeks, ginger and onion over a moderate heat, stirring from time to time, for 7–8 minutes. Stir in the salt and black pepper and then spoon the contents of the sauté pan into the milk in the casserole, spooning the mixture evenly around the meat.

Add the chopped Bramley apple and the chunks of Jerusalem artichokes. Cover the casserole with its lid or loosely cover the deep roasting tin with baking parchment, and cook in a moderately high oven (200°C / 400°F / gas 6) for 1 hour, then reduce the heat to moderate (180°C / 350°F / gas 4) and continue to cook, the pan uncovered now, for another 1½ hours.

Lift the casserole or deep roasting tin out of the oven. Carefully spoon the vegetables into a food processor and whiz to a smooth, thick puree. Dilute the puree with the milk from the roasting, taste, and add more salt and black pepper if you think it is needed.

Lift the meat from the roasting tin onto a large board and, with a sharp carving knife, cut the meat from the bones. Slice thickly, and serve one slice per person, on warmed plates, with a good spoonful of the thick pureed vegetables and apple on each serving.

Horseradish mash

Boil the potatoes in salted water until tender. Drain, and shake the pan over heat, to dry the cooked potatoes. Take the pan off the heat.

Put the milk, butter, salt, black pepper and nutmeg into a small saucepan and heat the milk until the butter melts.

Mash the cooked potatoes very thoroughly. Then, switching from masher to a wooden spoon, gradually add the melted butter and milk, beating the mashed potatoes very well. When all the milk and butter are incorporated, beat in the horseradish sauce, and dish up from the saucepan into a warmed dish.

The mash keeps warm at a low temperature very satisfactorily, the dish covered with foil.

For the horseradish mash

Serves 6

900g / 2lb potatoes (my choice is always for Rooster variety), weighed when peeled and cut into even-sized chunks

450ml / ¾ pint milk

50g / 2oz butter

1 tsp salt, about 10 grinds black pepper

A grating of nutmeg

2 tsp good horseradish sauce

Roast Saddle of Wild Boar with Shallot, Lemon and Apple Cream Sauce

Serves 6

900g / 2lb saddle of wild boar, trimmed of any small sections of membrane

12 rashers top-quality unsmoked streaky bacon

Black pepper

2–3 tbsp olive or rapeseed oil

The saddle is the most tender part of the animal, and has the potential to be dry when cooked. Wrapping it in best-quality streaky bacon and roasting the boned saddle prevents this. It goes very well with the creamy sauce, containing cooking apples which obligingly fall into a soft mush on cooking, their delicious taste spiked by diced fried shallots, lemon and horseradish. The horseradish mashed potatoes make a wonderful accompaniment to this dish, along with a steamed green vegetable, either purple sprouting or ordinary broccoli, or green beans.

Line a roasting tin with a sheet of baking parchment – this is just to make washing-up easier and quicker later on.

On a board, elongate each bacon rasher by stroking down its length with the blade of a knife.

Season the saddle with black pepper, and rub the olive oil into the meat. Wrap the saddle in the streaky bacon rashers and put the meat onto the parchment-lined roasting tin.

Roast in a hot oven (200°C / 400°F / gas 6) for 35–40 minutes. If the bacon looks a bit anaemic, blast it all over with a blowtorch to crisp it up.

Lift the saddle onto a warmed serving plate and cover loosely with foil to keep in the heat. Let it rest for 10–15 minutes before slicing the bacon-wrapped saddle to serve with the sauce alongside.

Creamy Apple, Shallot and Lemon Sauce

Melt the butter in a saucepan and fry the shallots for about 5 minutes. Then add the chopped apples to the shallots in the pan, cover the pan with its lid and cook over a moderate heat until the apple is soft, about 10–15 minutes. Beat the grated lemon rind, juice, horseradish, salt, black pepper and cream into the soft apples and shallots, replace the pan on the heat and simmer gently until you are ready to serve.

Serve either in a jug separately or spooned over the sliced wild boar saddle.

For the creamy apple, shallot and lemon sauce

Serves 6

4 banana shallots, skinned and finely diced

50g / 2oz butter

3 Bramley cooking apples, peeled, cored and chopped

Finely grated rind of 1 lemon

Juice of 1/2 lemon

1 tsp horseradish sauce

300ml / 1/2 pint double cream

1 tsp salt, about 10 grinds black pepper

Wild Boar Goulash

Serves 6

900g / 2lb trimmed wild boar meat, cut from the leg, cut into even-sized chunks about 2cm / 1" in size

4–5 tbsp olive oil

2 onions, skinned and very finely sliced

2 fat cloves garlic, skinned and finely diced

6 red peppers, halved and de-seeded, then sliced very finely

2 rounded tsp smoked paprika

1 tsp salt, about 20 grinds black pepper

6 tbsp crème fraiche or soured cream

Goulash is a wonderful dish, under-appreciated in the UK. It can be made with either beef, pork or venison – nicest with pork in my estimation, BUT if you can get hold of some wild boar, then that is the meat which makes THE most delicious goulash! The main ingredients for goulash are red peppers and paprika. If you can, use smoked paprika, for an increased depth of flavour – it is easily found on the delicatessen shelves in good supermarkets. A swirl of crème fraiche or soured cream on each serving adds the final touch to the flavours within a goulash. If you like, you can serve the goulash with mashed potatoes or boiled rice, but best of all is a dish of cheese-sauced pasta. Yes, I know that this sounds like real cold-weather comfort food, but that is exactly what it is meant to be. The red peppers and onions within the goulash provide great nutritional benefits, there is no flour or thickener in the sauce, and a helping of creamy cheese pasta is an absolutely delicious accompaniment.

In a large casserole heat the oil and, in small amounts at a time, brown the chunks of wild boar meat thoroughly on all sides, lifting the meat as it browns into a warm dish. When all the meat is browned, lower the heat beneath the casserole and fry the sliced onions, stirring occasionally to be sure of even cooking, for 5–6 minutes until soft and transparent. Lift them from the casserole into the dish with the boar meat. Add the sliced red peppers, and cook for 10–12 minutes, stirring occasionally so that they cook evenly. Then stir in the diced garlic and the paprika, mixing well.

Return the onions and browned wild boar meat to the casserole, mix all thoroughly, adding the salt and black pepper. Cover the casserole with its lid and cook in a low to moderate oven (150°C / 300°F / gas 3) for 1 hour 45 minutes. Take the casserole out of the oven, mix the contents well, then leave to cool. Store in a cold larder or the fridge for 36–48 hours.

Bring the casserole into room temperature half an hour before reheating on top of the cooker for 15 minutes, then in a low to moderate oven (150°C / 300°F / gas 3) for 30–35 minutes. Serve with a tablespoonful of crème fraiche (full or half fat, whichever you prefer) on top of each serving.

NB: You will see that there is no liquid in this recipe – that is deliberate. The cooked red peppers provide some juices, but it is meant to be a fairly dry goulash.

Creamy Cheese Pasta

Melt the butter in a saucepan and stir in the flour. Cook for a couple of minutes, adding the Dijon mustard at this stage, before gradually adding the milk, stirring all the time. When all the milk is incorporated, stir until the sauce simmers gently, and cook for a minute. Take the pan off the heat and stir in the salt, black pepper, nutmeg and cheddar cheese. Stir until the cheese melts completely. Then mix the drained, cooked pasta thoroughly through the sauce. Tip the contents of the pan into an ovenproof dish. Scatter the grated parmesan evenly over the surface. Bake in a moderate oven (180°C / 350°F / gas 4) for 35–40 minutes, or until the parmesan cheese on the surface has formed a golden crust. Serve to accompany the goulash.

For the creamy cheese pasta

Serves 6

375g / 12oz short pasta of your choice, boiled in salted water for 7 minutes, then drained and mixed with 1 tbsp olive oil.

50g / 2oz butter

50g / 2oz flour

1 tsp Dijon mustard (this doesn't taste mustardy in the sauce, but it enhances the flavour of the cheese)

750ml / 1¼ pint milk

1 tsp salt, about 15 grinds black pepper, a grating of nutmeg

75g / 3oz grated cheddar cheese (or Lancashire cheese if you can get it)

75g / 3oz grated parmesan

Carbonnade of Wild Boar

Serves 6

900g / 2lb trimmed wild boar meat, cut into even-sized chunks about 2cm / 1" in size

1 rounded tbsp flour mixed with 1 tsp salt, about 20 grinds black pepper, a good grating of nutmeg

3–4 tbsp olive or rapeseed oil

4 onions, skinned and finely sliced

600ml / 1 pint beer of your choice

300ml / ½ pint good stock (game or vegetable)

French bread sliced to an even thickness of 1cm, brushed on one side with olive oil and on the other side spread lightly with Dijon mustard

This method of cooking meat is more usually associated with beef, but a carbonnade is every bit as good, if not better, when wild boar is used instead. The beer used in the recipe can be whichever appeals to you. The crusty French bread slices which form the top of the carbonnade are brushed with olive oil on one side – the upper side – and spread lightly with Dijon mustard on the side pressed down amongst the meat. Serve with a green vegetable such as Savoy cabbage, broccoli or Brussels sprouts.

Put the chunks of wild boar meat into a large polythene bag with the seasoned flour, close the bag and shake it vigorously, to coat each bit of meat with the flour.

Heat the oil in a large casserole and, in relays, brown the floured chunks of meat on all sides. As the meat is browned, lift it onto a warm dish. Once all the meat is browned, reduce the heat beneath the casserole and fry the onions, stirring from time to time, for 8–10 minutes. Then replace the browned meat in amongst the onions, and add the beer and stock, stirring until the liquid simmers. Cover the casserole and cook in a moderate oven (180°C / 350°F / gas 4) for 1 hour, from simmering.

Cool, and store in a cold larder or the fridge for 36–48 hours. To finish off the carbonnade before serving, bring the casserole into room temperature for half an hour. Reheat on top of the cooker just until the sauce around the meat simmers. Then put the prepared slices of French bread, mustard sides down, into the contents of the casserole. The entire surface should be covered. Bake in the same moderate heat as for the first cooking (180°C / 350°F / gas 4) for 40–45 minutes or until the surface of the French bread is golden and light brown. Keep the casserole warm at a low temperature until ready to serve.

WILD DUCK

The words 'wild duck' in fact cover several species. Teal, wigeon and mallard are the three most usually eaten, with mallard being the most common. Mallard are the largest wild duck, and are to be found on the shelves of many supermarkets and in all poulterers and game dealers, whereas it is rare to be able to buy teal or wigeon, although a good game dealer would procure them for you if you specified them as a request. Unlike domestic duck, wild duck have virtually no fat, yet there is a most delicious richness of flavour which combines well with a number of other foods. Wild duck shot in coastal areas, where they eat plants growing near the sea, including seaweed, can have a flavour reflecting their diet. By roasting them with half a skinned onion or shallot inside their cavity you can eliminate this not entirely pleasant taste. And if you like, put a quartered orange, minus skin, inside the cavity with the onion/shallot. Recipes for delicious stews and casseroles using wild duck abound, and if you roast the birds, then it is very worthwhile roasting two or three extra for making into a wild duck shepherd's pie – which is every bit as good as the traditional version made with leftover roast lamb. Potted wild duck, the flavours spiked with thyme, orange and Worcestershire sauce, makes a delicious first course, or main course accompanied by baked jacket potatoes and a mustardy vinaigrette-dressed mixed leaf salad.

Marmalade Roast Wild Duck with Orange and Shallot Sauce

The sauce can be made in advance and reheated before serving with the duck. The marmalade should be spread over the ducks halfway through their roasting time; if it is spread at the start of their roasting, it tends to scorch and the flavour isn't what it should be. A well-seasoned mash makes a perfect accompaniment, and steamed purple-sprouting broccoli or sliced green beans provide a complementary flavour.

Start by preparing the sauce. Put the sugar, pared orange rind and red wine vinegar into a small saucepan over heat. Shake the pan until every grain of sugar has dissolved in the vinegar as it heats, then boil fast until the liquid has reduced by two thirds, then take the pan off the heat and set aside.

Melt the butter and fry the finely diced shallots, stirring occasionally, for 5–7 minutes. Stir in the flour and cook for a couple of minutes before gradually adding in the red wine and stock, stirring until the sauce simmers. Simmer gently for 2–3 minutes. Stir in the salt and black pepper, the orange juice and the wine vinegar syrup, discarding the orange rind. Cover the pan and store in a cold place until required. Reheat to serve with the roast duck.

Put the mallard onto a roasting tin with half an onion or a whole shallot inside each bird, and rub olive or rapeseed oil over each. Cover loosely with baking parchment, to protect the breasts of the duck from direct heat. Roast in a hot oven (200°C / 400°F / gas 6) for 30 minutes.

Meanwhile, put the marmalade into a bowl and add the salt and black pepper, mix well. Take the roasting tin out of the oven, remove the parchment and spread the seasoned marmalade over the ducks. Return the tin to the oven and roast for a further 30 minutes. Remove it from the oven, cover loosely with foil and, before serving and using game shears or scissors, cut each duck in half lengthways.

Serve with the orange and shallot sauce.

Serves 6

3 mallard

2 onions, skinned and halved (or 3 banana shallots, skinned)

3 tbsp orange marmalade of your choice

1 tsp salt, about 15 grinds black pepper

For the sauce

1 tbsp demerara sugar

300ml / ½ pint red wine vinegar

Pared rind of 1 orange (use a potato peeler to pare the rind, to avoid any bitter white pith), plus its juice

4 banana shallots, each skinned and finely diced

50g / 2oz butter

1 tbsp flour

300ml / ½ pint red wine

450ml / ¾ pint stock (e.g. a good vegetable stock)

1 tsp salt, about 15 grinds black pepper

Wild Duck with Tomato and Orange

Serves 6

3 mallard

3–4 tbsp olive or rapeseed oil

3 onions, skinned and finely sliced

400g tin chopped tomatoes

300ml / ½ pint red wine

Finely grated rind of 2 oranges, and their flesh, the pith sliced from the oranges, then the segments, slicing in between the membrane in towards the centre of each orange

1 tsp salt, about 20 grinds black pepper

The flavours of tomato and orange are delicious with wild duck. Boiled basmati rice flavoured with finely grated orange rind, olive oil and finely chopped parsley makes a very good accompaniment, with a mixed leaf salad.

In a large casserole heat the olive oil and brown the ducks on all sides. Lift them onto a large plate when they are browned.

Fry the finely sliced onions, stirring occasionally, for 5–6 minutes, then add the chopped tomatoes, red wine, salt and black pepper. Stir in the finely grated orange rind, replace the browned ducks in the casserole, cover the casserole and cook in a moderate oven (180°C / 350°F / gas 4) for 1 hour. Take the casserole out of the oven, cool, then lift each duck out and onto a large board. Cut the meat from each duck, replacing it in amongst the sauce with the casserole. Store overnight in either a cold larder or the fridge.

Take the casserole into room temperature half an hour before serving. Add the orange segments to the contents of the casserole, and reheat on top of the cooker until the sauce simmers, then replace the lid and heat in a moderate oven (180°C / 350°F / gas 4) for 30 minutes.

Serve with basmati rice mixed with finely grated orange rind, two tablespoons of olive oil and the same amount of finely chopped parsley.

Stir-fried Wild Duck Breasts with Ginger, Spring Onions, Pistachios and Sherry

This is a dish which takes minutes to cook, and providing you have a sharp knife, only minutes in its preparation time too. Boiled basmati rice makes a perfect accompaniment, with a mixed leaf salad on the side.

Over a high heat, heat the olive oil in a wide sauté pan. Add the strips of duck breast and stir-fry until they are evenly cooked, about 3–4 minutes. Add the diced ginger and garlic and the sliced spring onions to the duck strips in the pan, and continue to stir-fry for a further 2–3 minutes before adding the sherry, salt, black pepper and the shelled pistachios. Cook, stirring, for a further minute or two, then serve, spooned on to or beside boiled and drained basmati rice.

Serves 6

3–4 tbsp olive oil

6 duck breasts, cut from 3 mallard, sliced into finger-thick strips

4cm / 2" length of root ginger, its skin pared off and the ginger diced finely (or grated if you prefer)

2 fat cloves garlic, skinned and finely diced

12 spring onions, trimmed at either end and sliced lengthways as thinly as possible

75g / 3oz unsalted pistachios, shelled

300ml / ½ pint medium-dry sherry

1 tsp salt, about 20 grinds black pepper

Potted Wild Duck

Serves 6

450g / 1lb leftover roast duck meat, cut into small chunks

220g / 8oz butter plus 50g / 2oz butter

1 fat clove garlic, skinned and chopped

2 tbsp Worcestershire sauce

Finely grated rind and juice of 1 orange

½ tsp salt, 20 grinds black pepper

This uses up leftover roast wild duck, but it is so good that it is worth roasting more birds than you need just to make this recipe. The duck meat is flavoured with orange and Worcestershire sauce, and sealed with clarified butter in the individual pots or ramekins. I like to serve it with Melba toast, or with good oatcakes.

Put the 220g / 8oz butter into a saucepan on the lowest heat possible, or even on a radiator, to let the butter melt very, very slowly – this is for the clarified butter.

Melt the 50g / 2oz butter and fry the diced garlic for a minute.

Put the duck meat into a food processor and add the butter and garlic, the Worcestershire sauce, grated orange rind and juice, salt and black pepper. Whiz briefly, to pulverise the duck meat and to combine the contents of the processor but not to puree everything.

Divide evenly between 6 small pots or ramekins. Smooth over the surface of each.

Carefully pour only the surface of the clarified butter onto each pot or ramekin, leaving the white curd of the butter in the bottom of the saucepan. Leave each pot to set. Then cover each pot or ramekin with clingfilm and store them in the fridge until required.

Take the pots into room temperature for half an hour before serving, to lose the taste-numbing fridge chill. They will keep for up to 3 days in the fridge.

Wild Duck Shepherd's Pie with Celeriac Mash

This is such a good dish, and it is well worthwhile roasting more ducks than you will need just to have leftover duck meat for this pie. The combination of celeriac and potatoes in the mash adds a delicious taste dimension, and the only other accompaniment required is a green vegetable, perhaps steamed Brussels sprouts or broccoli. You can adjust the diced carrots and parsnips and add more of both if you have a rather meagre amount of leftover duck meat.

Heat the oil in a large casserole and fry the diced onions, carrots and parsnips together over a moderately high heat. Add the pared orange rind, and stir from time to time for 8–10 minutes, or until the vegetables are tender. Then stir in the pulverised duck meat, mix very well, and add the tomato puree and stock. Stir in the salt and black pepper, redcurrant jelly and the Worcestershire sauce. Bring the contents of the casserole to a gentle simmer, cover with the lid, and cook in a low to moderate oven (150°C / 300°F / gas 3) for 45 minutes. Take the casserole out of the oven and cool.

To make the topping, melt the butter in the milk, add the seasonings, then gradually beat the buttery milk into the mashed potatoes and celeriac.

Remove the orange rind from the cooled shepherd's pie. Spoon over the mash evenly, then with a fork make even lines down the length of the mash.

To cook, put the pie into a moderate oven (180°C / 350°F / gas 4) for 45–50 minutes. The surface of the mash should be speckled golden brown and the duck meat mixture just bubbling at the sides of the dish.

Serves 6

For the pie filling

675–900g / 1½–2lb leftover roast duck meat, cut into small chunks and briefly whizzed in a food processor to the texture of mince (take care not to whiz to a paste!)

3–4 tbsp olive or rapeseed oil

2 onions, skinned and neatly diced

3 carrots, trimmed, peeled and diced

3 parsnips, trimmed, peeled and diced

2 tbsp tomato puree

600ml / 1 pint vegetable stock

2 tbsp Worcestershire sauce

1 tsp redcurrant jelly

½ tsp salt, about 20 grinds black pepper

Pared rind of 1 orange (use a potato peeler to avoid any bitter white pith)

For the potato and celeriac topping

450g / 1lb each of peeled potatoes and peeled chunks of celeriac, boiled together in salted water until both are tender, then drained, steam dried over heat, and mashed very well.

300ml / ½ pint milk

50g / 2oz butter

1 tsp salt, about 10 grinds black pepper

A good grating of nutmeg

Roast Wild Duck with Lime and Gin Sauce

Serves 6

3 mallard

3 tbsp olive oil

1 onion, skinned and halved

For the sauce

50g / 2oz butter

4 banana shallots, skinned and finely diced

Grated rind and juice of 3 limes (keep them at room temperature – they will yield so much more juice)

1 tsp grain mustard

2 tbsp apricot jam

1 tbsp tomato puree

1 tsp white wine vinegar

1 rounded tsp arrowroot slaked with 300ml / ½ pint stock (I use vegetable stock for this)

150ml / ¼ pint gin

1 tsp salt, about 15 grinds black pepper

This is a most delicious sauce to serve with roast wild duck. You can make it a day in advance of serving, and reheat it to serve, if that is more convenient for you. The flavours within the sauce complement the taste of wild duck extremely well. I like to make baked sliced potatoes and onions – Potatoes Anna as they are called – to serve with this, and also any green leafy vegetable, such as kale, Savoy cabbage or broccoli.

Melt the butter in a saucepan and fry the shallots over a moderately high heat, stirring occasionally, for 5–6 minutes. Stir in the lime rinds and juices, apricot jam, grain mustard, tomato puree and white wine vinegar. Simmer the contents of the pan gently for 2–3 minutes before adding the arrowroot and stock, salt and black pepper. Stir until the sauce simmers again and cook for 5 minutes, simmering gently. Just before serving, stir in the gin.

To roast the wild ducks, put them onto a roasting tin and put half an onion inside the cavity of each duck. Rub a tablespoon of olive oil into each duck. Cover the ducks loosely with baking parchment and roast in a hot oven (200°C / 400°F / gas 6) for 1 hour. Take the roasting tin out of the oven, cover with foil to keep in their heat, and just before serving either carve the duck meat or, easier, cut each duck in half lengthways using game shears or heavy-duty scissors.

Wild Duck with Grapes and Paprika

This is a most delicious and unusual dish, and convenient too in that it can be made a day in advance of eating, stored overnight in a cold larder or the fridge. (In which case, don't add the sour cream until you reheat the dish.) Serve with very well beaten mashed potatoes and roast leeks and carrots as accompaniments.

Put the ducks into a roasting tin and put half an onion inside each bird. Pour the cider and water around the ducks in the roasting tin, add the salt and black pepper and cover the roasting tin with foil. Cook in a hot oven (200°C / 400°F / gas 6) for 1½ hours – they need a longer cooking time because foil, whilst useful as a lid, is a rotten conductor of heat. If you cook the ducks in a large casserole with its own lid, then only cook the ducks for 1 hour.

When the cooking time is up, take the roasting tin or casserole out of the oven, cool, strain the liquid into a jug for the sauce, and cut the meat from the ducks as neatly as you can.

To make the sauce, melt the butter in a casserole intended to contain the finished duck and sauce, and fry the diced shallots over a moderately high heat, stirring occasionally, for 5–6 minutes. Reduce the heat beneath the casserole and stir in the paprika and flour – take care not to scorch the paprika as this adversely affects its flavour. Cook for a minute before stirring in the cider liquid from roasting the ducks, stirring until the sauce simmers. Simmer gently for a couple of minutes, then add the salt, black pepper and halved grapes. Cool. Put the duck meat into the casserole, cover and store in a cold larder or the fridge until thirty minutes before reheating. Bring the cold casserole into room temperature for 30 minutes, then reheat on top of the cooker, until the sauce reaches simmering. Simmer very gently for 10–15 minutes, then stir the sour cream through the contents of the casserole 2 minutes before serving.

Serves 6

3 mallard

1 onion, skinned and halved

600ml / 1 pint dry cider mixed with 300ml / ½ pint water

1 tsp salt, 20 grinds black pepper

For the sauce

75g / 3oz butter

4 shallots, skinned and finely diced

1 rounded tbsp flour

2 tbsp paprika (use smoked paprika if you prefer)

The reserved liquid from cooking the ducks

1 tsp salt, about 15 grinds black pepper

375g / 12oz black grapes, halved (preferably seedless and if possible the really black grapes as opposed to the dark red ones)

300ml / ½ pint soured cream

Braised Wild Duck with Plums, Shallots and Cinnamon

Serves 6

3 mallard, 2 will suffice if they are both drakes.

1 orange cut into 3 sections – skin on – and cut in half if you are using 2 birds.

6 banana shallots, each skinned and quartered lengthways

3 tbsp olive oil

675g / 1½lbs ripe plums, each cut in half and twisted in opposite directions, and the stones removed. Each plum-half then cut in half.

½ teaspoon ground cinnamon – no more

1 teaspoon salt, about 20 grinds of black pepper

300ml / ½ pint freshly squeezed orange juice – a good bought brand will do instead.

The cinnamon is the merest hint of this wonderful spice which, if used too enthusiastically can overpower all the other flavours in the dish. But cinnamon combined with plums – and any variety of plum is suitable for this dish, with the sole exception of Victorias. Victoria plums are the best of all varieties to eat, but when cooked, they take on a bland taste which only disappoints. I like to strip the cooked meat from the duck carcases after cooking. That makes the dish so much easier to serve, and for your guests to eat.

This is good with crispy pieces of roast potato with rosemary, and with sliced roast courgettes with garlic, but any steamed green vegetable is delicious with the duck in its unctuous plum and shallot sauce.

Heat the oil in a wide pan and brown the ducks on all sides. Lift them onto a plate as they are browned.

Add the quartered shallots to the hot oil in the pan, and, over a moderately high heat, fry the shallots until they are soft, about 5 minutes. Add the quartered plums to the shallots, and the salt and black pepper. Stir well, and then stir in the cinnamon and orange juice. Replace the ducks in the pan, pushing them down amongst the plums and shallots, Cover the pan with its lid and cook in a moderate heat (350°F / 180°C / gas 4) for 1 hour 15 minutes. Take the pan out of the oven and cool. When cool enough to handle the ducks without scorching your fingers, lift each out onto a board and remove the flesh, taking care not to let any bones slip back in amongst the meat. Replace all meat in the pan with the plums and shallots, and when cold store in the fridge.

To reheat, take the pan into room temperature for half an hour, then reheat on top of the cooker until the mixture just simmers. Re-cover the pan and cook in the same moderate temperature as for the initial cooking, for 15 minutes after reaching simmering.

WOODCOCK AND SNIPE

Woodcock are migratory. They arrive on the first full moon in November – in Skye, anyway – and they love frosty weather. Snipe live in bogs, year round. Woodcock are magical, elusive birds, and there are people for whom roast woodcock is a delicacy above all other game delicacies, and Godfrey, my husband, is one of these people. It may be deemed old-fashioned by some, but for Godfrey and others for whom roast woodcock is a rare treat, they must be eaten with their 'trail' (i.e. innards) intact. And their brains. These woodcock lovers know just how to spot the 'gritty bag' (i.e. the stomach). Snipe are eaten in the same way. The Jack Snipe are the smallest of the species, and they are protected throughout the British Isles, but other types of snipe are deemed game birds and good for eating.

Both woodcock and snipe are roasted draped in best-quality thinly sliced streaky bacon – unsmoked – and served on butter-brushed baked bread, with gravy and game chips. The perfect accompaniment to both roast woodcock and roast snipe is a watercress salad.

Roast Woodcock (or Snipe)

Melt the butter in a small roasting tin, large enough to accommodate the number of woodcock to feed your family or friends. Brush either side of each slice of crustless bread with the melted butter, then turn each woodcock in the melted butter, leaving them upright, on each baked buttered slice of bread. Cover each woodcock (or snipe) with streaky bacon. Scatter salt and grind black pepper over all. Roast in a hot oven (220°C / 450°F / gas 7) for 30 minutes.

Serve the woodcock (or snipe) accompanied by game chips (see p.26) and gravy (see p.31), plus a watercress salad.

I bird serves I person

Per bird, allow:

50g / 2oz butter

2 rashers streaky bacon

I slice white bread, crusts removed, bread brushed with melted butter then baked in a hot oven (see the recipe on p.29)

½ tsp salt, 10–15 grinds black pepper

Roast Woodcock or Snipe on a bed of Beetroot and Shallots

Serves 6

6 birds, either woodcock or snipe

6 rashers of unsmoked, thinly cut streaky bacon

900g / 2lbs beetroot, weighed before peeling

6 banana shallots, each skinned, halved lengthways and finely diced

2–3 tbsp olive oil

I tsp salt, about 20 grinds of black pepper

A sprig of thyme, approximately 6 cm long, the tiny leaves stripped from the stalks

The treat of woodcock or snipe for those who love eating them is that the entire bird is eaten, the brain and 'trail'. The danger in being too innovative in cooking these small birds is to include foods that overpower their flavour. But I think that beetroot enhances their taste, and when the birds are roasted on top of the diced beetroot and shallots the resulting dish needs no bread sauce or gravy to complete it. Accompany the birds with pureed roast carrots and parsnips, and, if you like, also a green vegetable such as broccoli or purple sprouting.

Peel the beetroot using a potato peeler, then cut each beetroot in half, slice across each half, then slice down, to give neat dice about fingernail size.

Put the diced beetroot into a roasting tin with the diced shallots. Add the olive oil, thyme, salt and black pepper, and, with your hands, mix thoroughly. Roast in a hot oven (400°F / 200°C / gas 6) for 30 minutes. Take the roasting tin out, stir up the diced beetroot and shallots, and spread evenly before putting the birds on top of the vegetables. Cut each bacon rasher in half – using scissors – and put two halves on top of each bird. Put the roasting tin and its contents back into the oven and cook for 35–40 minutes, or for 40–45 minutes if you prefer your birds cooked through with no tinge of pink. Take the roasting tin out of the oven, cover with foil and leave to stand for 10 minutes before serving.

There are other excellent accompaniments for this dish which contribute a contrasting crunchy texture to that of the soft braised birds on their bed of diced shallots and beetroot. Sauteed small chunks of potato, roasted in olive oil or goosefat, their flavour spiked with sprigs of thyme – to be removed before serving – is delicious, or alternatively, game chips are equally good if a crunchy texture contrast is being sought. And a dish of rowan jelly handed separately introduces another taste enhancer for the woodcock or snipe. So simple though this dish is, the enhancements are both varied and give you a wide choice.

Roast Woodcock or Snipe on a Bed of Shallots, Bacon and Potatoes

Serves 6

6 woodcock or snipe

8 rashers of unsmoked back bacon, the rim of fat trimmed off – easiest done with scissors – and the bacon sliced into strips

6 banana shallots, each skinned and sliced into 4 lengthways

750g / 1½ lbs potatoes – I prefer the Rooster variety to any other for this and most other potato recipes – weighed after peeling, and the potatoes then cut into cubes approx. 1 centimetre in size

3 tbsp olive oil plus 50g / 2oz butter

1 tsp salt, about 20 grinds of black pepper

A grating of nutmeg

300ml / ½ pint double cream

This recipe is delicious, and either woodcock or snipe work equally well cooked this way, roast breast down amongst the potato, bacon and shallot mixture. This keeps them moist, and in turn, they impart their flavour throughout the vegetables and bacon – all the tastes are so mutually complementary. A steamed green vegetable such as sliced green beans, chopped kale or brussels sprouts completes this main course.

Start by cooking the potato mixture – heat the olive oil and melt the butter together in a wide sauté pan, and add the quartered shallots and the bacon strips. Cook, stirring occasionally, for about 5 minutes, or until the shallots look almost transparent. Then add the cubed potatoes to the contents of the pan. Season with salt, black pepper and nutmeg, and fry, stirring occasionally, until the potatoes soften. Pour in the double cream. This will take about 30 minutes, so be prepared! The potatoes do not have to be cooked right through during this time, because they will continue cooking with the birds.

Push the snipe or woodcock breast down in amongst the creamy potato mixture. Cover the surface with baking parchment, and cook in a moderate heat (350°F / 180°C / gas 4) for 40–45 minutes.

VENISON

Venison is widely available the length and breadth of the United Kingdom. Venison is a lean red meat, and widely useful in all its varying cuts, but hanging the meat is essential, both for flavour and for tenderness.

Venison comes from differing species of deer. The most commonly found is that from red deer, both hinds (female) and stags (male). Venison from roe deer – whether from a buck (male) or a doe (female) – is a more delicate meat, and less commonly available. Fillet of roe needs less cooking time than that from red deer. Other varieties of deer are sika, which tend to have a very thin rim of fat beneath their coat, and muntjac.

For my taste, wild deer provide much better flavour than farmed deer. The recipes within this chapter are for venison from red deer, but any other variety can be substituted. For any other variety of deer, judge the cooking time by the weight of the meat used.

No amount of marinating or careful cooking can make a roast haunch of red deer anything other than dry. But a haunch of roe deer or sika can be delicious.

Those who aren't used to eating venison fear it will have a strong taste. They have no need of such fear. Venison has a most interesting flavour, and one which makes delicious stews, casseroles and roasts. If you fear tough meat, then steep the venison in milk overnight. Milk is the single-ingredient marinade which both tenderises and draws out the strong flavour of the meat. The milk must be drained away after marinating, the meat patted dry with kitchen paper before being cut up for cooking. I first discovered the efficacy of milk as a marinade when, about 40 years ago, I was given the liver from a stag. I was instructed to steep it in milk overnight, which I did, and the donor then requested fried slices of the stag's liver fried for his breakfast. It smelled delicious! Conversely, Godfrey remembers with horror when he was a boy and staying with a friend, being given by his hostess sandwiches with elderly stag's liver as the filling!

Within this chapter are recipes for pasta, using venison sausagemeat; for venison fillet encased in puff pastry, Wellington-style; for venison shin cooked with tomatoes, onions and celery and served with boiled basmati rice with gremolata, among numerous different ways to casserole this fantastic meat. There is a recipe for venison paté, which contains some venison liver, and for a venison pasty, excellent for wrapping in foil and being tucked into a deep pocket for a picnic during a long day out on the hill. There is a recipe for air-dried wafer-thin slices of venison which is very good with the accompanying salad containing pears and walnuts.

I hope, within this chapter, to encourage all those who have never before eaten venison to go out and buy some, and to find a new, delicious and nutritious addition to their diet!

Roast Fillet of Venison with Port, Redcurrant Jelly and Green Peppercorn Sauce

Serves 6

900g / 2lb venison fillet, trimmed of any membrane

3–4 tbsp olive oil

1 tsp salt, 10–15 grinds black pepper

This is a dish for a special occasion. And it is a convenient dish, because the sauce can be made entirely in advance, and reheated before serving in a bowl or jug to accompany the sliced roast venison fillet. Venison fillet is a fairly thin cut of meat and you will see in the recipe that I sear it on all sides then roast it for just 10 minutes in a very hot oven. If you prefer your meat more red than pink, reduce the roasting time to 5 minutes after searing the fillet.

Mix salt, pepper and olive oil together. Rub the seasoned oil thoroughly into the trimmed venison fillet.

Heat a large sauté pan and sear the oiled meat on all sides. Then put the seared meat into a roasting tin and roast in a hot oven (220°C / 450°F / gas 7) for 10 minutes for pink meat, or 5 if you prefer your fillet really rare. When the roasting time is up, take the tin out of the oven, cover entirely with foil to keep in the heat, and leave the meat to rest for 10–15 minutes before lifting on to a large board to slice. Arrange the slices on a warmed serving plate and cover with foil until you ready to serve, accompanied by green peppercorn and ginger and port sauce (see p.32).

Venison Shank Ossobuco Style, with Gremolata Rice

In Italy, Ossobuco is made with veal shin. But I have often made it with venison shin, and I think it tastes even better! Venison shin is smaller than a piece of veal shin, so you do need to allow more slices per person. I always take the meat off the bones after the initial cooking, as it makes the dish so much easier to eat, and allows you, the cook, to discard the bones and any bits of gristle you encounter. Be sure to push the marrow from the centre of each slice of venison shin – the shin is sliced across, and each slice will have some marrow in the centre of the bone, which is the 'buco' – the hole – in the title of the dish.

Serves 6

8–12 slices venison shin (depends on the size of the animal)

4–5 tbsp olive oil

3 onions, skinned thinly sliced

4 sticks celery, trimmed, peeled with a potato peeler to remove the stringy bits, then very thinly sliced

1–2 fat cloves garlic, skinned and finely diced

3 x 400g tins chopped tomatoes

1 tsp salt, about 20 grinds black pepper

½ tsp sugar

Heat the olive oil in a large casserole and brown the slices of venison shin on each side. Once browned, lift them onto a warm plate.

Lower the heat slightly beneath the casserole and fry the onions and celery, stirring from time to time, for 6–8 minutes until the onions are soft and transparent. Then add the chopped tomatoes, salt, black pepper and sugar. Stir well, heat until simmering, then return the pieces of browned venison shin to the pan, pushing them down amongst the tomatoes, onions and celery in the casserole.

Bring the tomatoes back to simmering, cover with the lid, and cook in a low moderate oven (150°C / 300°F / gas 3) for 2½ hours. The meat should be almost falling from the bones, and the rich tomato sauce will be infused with flavour from the venison. Cool the casserole, then lift out each slice of shin and carefully remove the meat from the bones, discarding the bones and any gristle. Be sure to push the jelly-like marrow from the centre of each slice of bone. Put the meat and marrow back into the casserole and mix both into the tomato sauce. Store the casserole, covered, in either a cold larder or the fridge, for up to 36 hours.

For the gremolata rice

Serves 6

375–450g / 12oz–1lb basmati rice

Finely grated rind of 1 lemon

3 tbsp extra virgin olive oil

1 tsp salt, about 10 grinds black pepper

1 fat clove garlic, skinned and very finely diced

2 tbsp finely chopped parsley (either flat or curly leaved, it doesn't matter)

To reheat before serving, take the casserole into room temperature for half an hour. Then reheat on top of the cooker, until the sauce just simmers. Replace the lid, and cook in a moderate oven (180°C / 350°F / gas 4) for 30 minutes. Serve with gremolata rice.

Gremolata Rice

Boil the rice in salted water until tender – about 10 minutes. Drain the rice in a large sieve under running hot water to rinse, then shake the sieve gently and put the cooked rice into a warm serving dish. Mix thoroughly with the other ingredients and serve.

Venison Casseroled with Prunes and Pickled Walnuts

This is one of my oldest venison recipes, and one I still love and make fairly regularly, almost five decades since I first made it when I was an extremely inexperienced novice cook at the Traverse Theatre in Edinburgh! The reason this recipe has endured so successfully is because the sharp and sweet flavours in the pickled walnuts and prunes are so exactly right with the flavour of venison, and all the tastes mellow as the casserole is cooked, cooled and reheated before serving. Twice cooking is almost obligatory for casseroles; the flavours are vastly better than if a casserole is made and eaten straight away. This needs to be accompanied by well-beaten mashed potatoes and a green vegetable – e.g. Brussels sprouts or Savoy cabbage.

Serves 6

900g / 2lb venison, trimmed of any membrane and cut into 2cm / 1" chunks

1 rounded tbsp flour

1 tsp salt, about 25 grinds black pepper

4 tbsp olive or rapeseed oil

2 onions, skinned and finely sliced

6 pickled walnuts, halved

12 soft prunes, halved

300ml / ½ pint red wine

600ml / 1 pint stock (I use vegetable stock)

Heat the oil in a large casserole. Put the chunks of venison, flour, salt and black pepper into a large polythene bag and close the ends. Shake the bag hard, to coat each bit of meat in seasoned flour.

Brown the floured meat a small amount at a time so that the heat within the casserole remains high. Brown the meat on all sides and, as it browns, lift it onto a warmed dish. When all the venison is browned, reduce the heat slightly beneath the casserole and fry the sliced onions, stirring from time to time, for 5–6 minutes until soft and transparent.

Return the browned meat to the casserole and add the red wine and stock, stirring all the time until the liquid simmers. Add the pickled walnuts and prunes, stir until simmering once more, then cover the casserole with its lid and cook in a moderate oven (180°C / 350°F / gas 4) for 1¼ hours. Take the casserole out of the oven, cool, and store in either a cold larder or the fridge for up to 36 hours.

Before reheating, take the casserole into room temperature for half an hour. Reheat on top of the cooker until the liquid simmers, then replace the lid and cook in the same moderate oven (180°C / 350°F / gas 4) for 25–30 minutes. Serve.

Air-dried or Smoked Sliced Venison with Pear, Fried Walnuts and Watercress Salad

Serves 6 as a first course

3 slices of venison per person

120g / 4oz chopped walnuts

1 tsp salt, 15 grinds black pepper

6 tbsp olive oil

4 ripe pears, quartered, peeled and cut into chunks

Juice of ½ lemon

120g / 4oz watercress, snipped with scissors

I hasten to note that this recipe does not involve you air-drying or smoking venison! But many enterprising families up and down Scotland are preserving thinly sliced venison by either air-drying or smoking it, and packages of both are to be found on the shelves of good delis and supermarkets across the country. I fear that if people don't buy them it's because they cannot think how to serve them. One way is as a first course, with a good dollop of chutney at the side, but this salad is my favourite way to serve such preserved venison. The olive oil-fried walnuts add a most delicious contrast of texture as well as their flavour to the salad, and the pears, walnuts and watercress all combine so very well with the flavour of the venison, whether it is smoked or air-dried.

Heat the olive oil in a wide pan and add the salt, black pepper and chopped walnuts. Over a moderately high heat fry the walnuts, stirring from time to time, for about 5 minutes. Then take the pan off the heat and cool.

Mix the pears, lemon juice and snipped watercress in a bowl. Mix in the contents of the cooled walnut pan, including all the oil, and combine thoroughly. Do this shortly before dividing the salad between the 6 plates of venison slices. Beware mixing the oil and walnuts into the watercress too far ahead of serving because the watercress will wilt if left in oil for any length of time.

Venison Sausagemeat Sauce for Pasta

This is a most sustaining and robust pasta sauce. Truly a winter warmer of a dish! Skin each sausage with the point of a sharp knife and peel off the skins – they slip off easily.

Heat the oil in a wide sauté pan and fry the onions, carrots and celery, stirring occasionally, for 10 minutes. Then add the garlic and the skinned sausages, both venison and pork, breaking up their shape with your wooden spoon, and mixing them into the vegetables as you do so. When the sausages are all broken and resemble mince, stir in the tomato puree, red wine and chopped tomatoes, salt and black pepper. Stir well, cover the pan with its lid, and simmer the contents very gently for 30–35 minutes. Then take the lid off the pan, and cook for a further 10–15 minutes.

Serve with cooked drained short pasta – penne would be my choice.

Serves 6

4 tbsp olive or rapeseed oil

2 onions, skinned and finely diced

4 sticks celery, trimmed, peeled with a potato peeler to remove the stringy bits, then finely sliced

2 medium carrots, trimmed, peeled and neatly diced

I fat clove garlic, skinned and diced

450g / Ilb venison sausages, skinned

220g / 8oz pork sausages, skinned

I tbsp tomato puree

300ml / 1/2 pint red wine

400g tin chopped tomatoes

I tsp salt, about 20 grinds black pepper

Venison Liver with Onions and Bacon

Serves 6

1 venison liver (there won't be very much liver per person, but the onions, bacon, potatoes and spinach make for very good accompaniments)

Milk to cover the liver

2 tbsp olive or rapeseed oil

50g / 2oz butter

For the spinach with onions, raisins and pinenuts

Serves 6

220g / 8oz young spinach leaves (this looks a vast amount, but it wilts right down on cooking)

2 tbsp olive oil

2 onions, skinned and neatly diced

50g / 2oz raisins

75g / 3oz pinenuts, dry fried in a frying pan to toast them light brown

1 tsp salt, about 15 grinds black pepper

For this dish to be really delicious, it is best if the liver is from a young beast. A dish of well-beaten mashed potatoes and some steamed spinach with raisins and toasted pinenuts complete this delicious meal – delicious, that is, for those of us who love liver.

Ease the thin membrane which encases the liver, and peel it off. Put the liver into a wide dish and cover with milk. Leave for several hours or overnight, covered, in a cold larder or the fridge.

Before cooking, drain the milk down the sink and pat the liver dry using kitchen paper. Put the liver onto a board and slice it evenly, trimming away any tubes you encounter within.

To cook, heat the oil and melt the butter together in a wide sauté pan. Fry the slices of liver briefly, for about 1 minute on each side. Serve with streaky bacon, well-beaten mashed potatoes and a dish of spinach with raisins and pinenuts.

Spinach with Onions, Raisins and Pinenuts

Put the spinach into a large saucepan and pour boiling water over it. Clamp a lid on the pan and cook for 2 minutes on a moderately high heat. When the spinach has wilted, drain off the water thoroughly and, when the spinach is cool enough to handle, squeeze all excess liquid from it. On a board, chop the wilted spinach.

Heat the olive oil in a saucepan and, over a moderate heat, fry the diced onions, stirring occasionally to make sure that they cook evenly, until soft and transparent. Then stir in the chopped spinach, raisins, salt and black pepper and mix well. Stir in the cooled toasted pinenuts, mix well, and tip the contents of the saucepan into a warmed serving dish to serve with the fried liver. Add baked rashers of streaky bacon, allowing 2–3 per person.

Venison Wellington

This is a special-occasion dish. But it is also a convenient dish because it can be prepared entirely several hours in advance of baking. I like to serve this with the red cabbage dish (see p. 24), and with sliced green beans and well-beaten mashed potatoes. A dish of rowan jelly is almost essential as an accompaniment, too.

Serves 6

320g packet all-butter puff pastry, rolled out

900g / 2lb piece venison fillet weighing about

2 tbsp olive oil

1 tsp salt, about 15 grinds black pepper

1 large egg, beaten in a small dish

Note that the mushrooms and venison must be completely cold before assembling the Wellington, so they must be prepared in advance.

Start by making the mushroom mixture. Heat the oil and melt the butter together in a wide sauté pan and, over a moderate heat, fry the onion and bacon for 3–4 minutes, then add the garlic and mushrooms, raise the heat beneath the pan and cook, stirring, until the mushrooms are soft and reduced in amount. Stir in the salt, black pepper and Madeira. Simmer until the Madeira has reduced away to nothing. Take the pan off the heat and cool completely.

To prepare the venison fillet, rub the olive oil, salt and black pepper all over the meat. Heat a dry sauté pan (no oil or butter required) and sear the fillet all over. Cool completely.

Lay the rolled-out puff pastry on a baking tray. Put the cooled, seared venison fillet onto this. Spoon the cooled mushroom mixture down the length of the fillet. Brush the entire edges of the puff pastry with beaten egg and fold the edges over lengthways, then the short ends, tucking them neatly under. Turn the pastry roll over so that the seam is underneath. Brush the entire pastry parcel with beaten egg and make a diamond pattern, with a sharp knife on the surface of the pastry, taking care not to cut right through the pastry. Cut in lines diagonally one way, then across the other way to achieve this diamond effect, the lines about 1cm apart.

For the mushroom and Madeira mixture to top the fillet beneath the pastry

2 tbsp olive oil

25g / 1oz butter

1 onion, skinned and finely diced

1 fat clove garlic, skinned and finely diced

450g / 1lb flat mushrooms, stalks removed, diced into thumbnail size

1 rasher top-quality back bacon, unsmoked, fat rimmed off and the bacon diced

½ tsp salt, about 15 grinds black pepper

150ml / ¼ pint Madeira

Leave the Wellington in a cold larder or the fridge until half an hour before baking. Take the Wellington in its baking tray into room temperature for 30 minutes, then bake in a hot oven (200°C / 400°F / gas 6) for 15 minutes, then reduce the heat to moderate (180°C / 350°F / gas 4) and cook for a further 25–30 minutes. The pastry should be golden-brown and puffed.

Remove the Wellington from the oven and let it stand, loosely covered with foil, for 10 minutes before carving into fat slices to serve.

Venison Stroganoff

This is such a delicious special-occasion dish, and it takes only minutes to cook, because everything can be prepared hours in advance. The sliced mushrooms don't deteriorate in the slightest by being roasted in advance. Note that you must use double cream for this recipe. Lower-fat cream won't thicken as it bubbles, and could curdle. Boiled basmati rice makes the perfect accompaniment, but stir a tablespoon of olive oil and some finely chopped parsley – about 2 tablespoons – through the cooked, drained rice before serving. This not only makes the rice look more appealing, it tastes more delicious. Add a green vegetable to complete the meal, either steamed Brussels sprouts or green beans.

Slice the meat into even-sized strips, about the size of a little finger. Put the sliced mushrooms onto a roasting tin. Add the olive oil, salt and black pepper and, with your hands, rub the oil into the sliced mushrooms. Spread in an even layer, and roast in a hot oven (200°C / 400°F / gas 6) for 35–40 minutes. Halfway through cooking time, take the roasting tin out of the oven and shuffle around the mushrooms, spreading them in an even layer having done so.

Tip the oil from around the mushrooms into a sauté pan. Over a high heat, stir-fry the strips of venison fillet for a couple of minutes, then add the garlic and the roast mushrooms, stir all together well, then add the double cream. Mix well, let the cream bubble for 2–3 minutes, then dish up the venison stroganoff into a warmed serving dish. Cover the dish loosely with foil and keep it warm in a low-temperature oven until you are ready to serve.

Serves 6

900g / 2lb venison fillet

675g / 1½ lb flat mushrooms, the stalks cut level with the caps and the mushrooms sliced evenly into slices about ½cm thick

3–4 tbsp olive oil

1 tsp salt, about 20 grinds black pepper

2 fat cloves garlic, skinned and finely diced

450ml / ¾ pint double cream

Venison Pasties

Serves 6

2 packets all-butter puff pastry, rolled out

2 large eggs, beaten in a small bowl

For the venison filling

4–5 tbsp olive or rapeseed oil

2 onions, skinned and finely diced

4 medium carrots, peeled and neatly diced

675g / 1½ lb minced venison

1 rounded tbsp flour

1 tbsp tomato puree

2 tbsp Worcestershire sauce

1 tsp redcurrant jelly

300ml / ½ pint red wine

300ml / ½ pint stock (use game stock or vegetable stock)

1 tsp salt, about 15 grinds black pepper

In the introduction to this chapter I mentioned that my husband, Godfrey, had once been given the most disgusting sandwiches imaginable, containing cold fried venison liver. Well, these venison pasties make the very opposite of such a picnic – they are delicious! They can be prepared the night before, needing only to be baked on the morning of the picnic. They are wrapped, individually, in foil, about 20 minutes after being taken from the oven.

Steam the diced carrots for 4–5 minutes, then drain on kitchen paper and cool.

Heat the oil in a casserole and brown the venison mince thoroughly. With a slotted spoon – and leaving behind as much of the oil as you can – lift the browned venison mince into a warm bowl. Then fry the diced onions for 4–5 minutes. Add the steamed and cooled diced carrots to the onions, and cook together for a further 4–5 minutes. Replace the browned venison mince in amongst the onions and carrots, mix well, and stir in the flour. Cook for a minute before stirring in the tomato puree, Worcestershire sauce, red wine, stock, redcurrant jelly, salt and black pepper. Stir until the mixture simmers gently. With the pan uncovered, simmer gently for 20–25 minutes. Cool.

To make up the pasties, lay the rolled-out pastry on to a lightly floured work surface. Cut each into 3 even-sized pieces. Brush around the edges of each with beaten egg. Put a spoonful of the cold minced venison onto each piece of pastry, dividing the venison mince evenly between the 6 strips of pastry and shaping the mixture into a neat oblong shape. Then fold the pastry over to form neat parcels.

Turn over each pasty, brush each thoroughly with beaten egg, make one small stab in the centre of each pastry and bake in a moderate oven (180°C / 350°F / gas 4) for 45–50 minutes, or until deep golden-brown and puffed. Take the tray out of the oven and cool for 20 minutes before wrapping each pasty loosely in foil.

Venison Casseroled with Shallots and Beetroot, Served with Parsley and Lemon Dumplings

This is a most sustaining and delicious dish. The beetroot helps to tenderise the venison, hence the quick cooking time. (Beetroot contains the same tenderising enzyme that is found in papaya.) The dumplings are full of flavour, and they are lighter if you use vegetarian suet, which has a much lower fat content than beef suet. The dumplings, which cook within the casserole, mean that for most people there is no need for potatoes. But I do like a green vegetable, such as steamed purple sprouting broccoli, or Brussels sprouts, or cabbage.

Put the chunks of venison into a large polythene bag with the flour, salt and black pepper. Close the bag and shake it hard, to coat each bit of meat with seasoned flour.

Heat the oil in a large casserole and, over a high heat, brown the floured chunks of venison on all sides, in relays. As the meat is browned, lift it onto a warm dish.

When all the venison is browned, reduce the heat slightly and fry the shallots, stirring occasionally, for 4–5 minutes. Then add the strips of beetroot to the shallots in the casserole, and fry for a further 5 minutes, stirring occasionally. Replace the browned venison in the casserole, and stir in the horseradish, red wine, stock and redcurrant jelly, stirring until the liquid simmers.

Cover the casserole with its lid and cook, from simmering, in a moderate oven (180°C / 350°F / gas 4) for 45 minutes. Take out of the oven, cool, and store for up to 36 hours either in a cold larder or the fridge.

Serves 6

900g venison, trimmed of any silvery membrane and cut into even-sized chunks, approx. 2cm / 1" size

1 rounded tbsp flour

1 tsp salt, 20 grinds black pepper

3–4 tbsp olive or rapeseed oil

9 banana shallots, skinned and finely sliced

4 beetroot, about apple sized, peeled and sliced into finger strips, or diced

1 tsp horseradish relish

300ml / ½ pint red wine

600ml / 1 pint stock (either game or vegetable stock)

1 tsp redcurrant jelly

For the dumplings

220g / 8oz self-raising flour

1 tsp salt, about 15 grinds black pepper

120g / 4oz vegetarian suet

Finely grated rind of 1 lemon

1 tbsp finely chopped parsley

Cold water, to mix to a dough

Meanwhile, make the dumplings. Sieve the flour, salt and black pepper into a bowl. Add the suet, lemon rind and chopped parsley, and mix all together thoroughly before adding just enough cold water to mix to a dough.

Between your floured hands, make the dough into small, even-sized balls – a bit bigger than a walnut but smaller than a golf ball. If you do these in advance, leave them on a sheet of baking parchment, loosely covered with clingfilm, until you are ready to cook them in the casserole. They are fine if left, covered, for several hours.

Before reheating, take the casserole into room temperature for half an hour. Reheat on top of the cooker until the gravy-like sauce reaches simmering, then drop in the dumplings, allow the sauce to simmer gently, and push the dumplings down into the contents of the casserole. Cover with the lid, and cook in the same moderate oven (180°C / 350°F / gas 4) for a further 30–35 minutes.

Potted Venison with Green Peppercorns

This is coarser than a paté, and it is sealed with clarified butter. It does require some venison liver, preferably from a young beast. The green peppercorns add a touch of piquancy to the venison meat and liver combination, and gives a delicious flavour. I like to serve it with either oatcakes or Melba toast.

Start by marinating the liver. Put it into a dish and immerse in milk. Leave in a cool place for several hours.

Meanwhile, heat 1 tablespoon of olive oil in a casserole or pan and brown the chunks of venison all over. Then add the chopped onion to the venison in the pan, and cook for a further 5–7 minutes, until the onion is soft and transparent. Add the port and stock, celery, bay leaves, redcurrant jelly, salt and black pepper. Bring the liquid to a gentle simmer, cover the pan and cook in a moderate oven (180°C / 350°F / gas 4) for 1 hour. Take the pan out of the oven and cool.

After several hours' marinating, drain the liver and pour the milk down the sink. Pat the liver dry with kitchen paper, trim it of all membrane and cut it into chunks. Heat the remaining tablespoon of olive oil in a small frying pan and fry the pieces of trimmed liver, stirring, for 1–2 minutes. Cool.

Put the butter into a saucepan on the lowest heat you can find – sit it on a radiator, or if you cook on a Raeburn or an Aga, put the pan at the back of the stove, not on direct heat. Let the butter melt very, very slowly – this is the easiest way to clarify butter.

To make the potted venison, lift the cooked meat from its liquid and put it into a food processor, with the liver and 2 tablespoons of the stock from the meat pan. Whiz briefly, to break up and combine the meat and liver but not to puree it. Scrape the pulverised venison and liver mixture from the processor into a bowl and mix in the green

Serves 6

450g / 1lb venison leg meat, cut into small chunks about 2cm / 1" in size

220g / 8oz venison liver (or you can substitute lamb's liver)

Enough milk to marinade the liver

2 tbsp olive oil

1 onion, skinned and chopped

1 stick celery, broken in half

2 bay leaves

300ml / ½ pint port

300ml / ½ pint stock (vegetable stock is fine for this)

1 tsp redcurrant jelly

1 tsp salt, about 15 grinds black pepper

2 tsp jarred green peppercorns, drained of their preserving brine

220g / 8oz butter

peppercorns thoroughly (don't put the peppercorns into the processor). Divide this mixture between 6 ramekins.

Carefully pour the melted butter from the saucepan on top of each ramekin, leaving the white curdy part of the milk in the base of the saucepan. Leave the butter-covered ramekins until cold, then clingfilm each and store in the fridge until required – they will keep well for up to 3 days. Take them into room temperature half an hour before serving.

Venison and Ale Puff Pastry Pie

A pie is inevitably greeted with glee – and venison is such a perfect meat for a pie. The ale can be of your choosing – the Black Isle Brewery makes a delicious range and so too does the Isle of Skye Brewery. But there are so many excellent breweries all around the United Kingdom, so choose one close to where you live. I never think that potatoes are necessary with a pie, but mashed celeriac is a very good accompaniment, along with a steamed green veg, such as purple sprouting broccoli, Savoy cabbage or Brussels sprouts. And a dish of rowan jelly completes the perfection of this main course.

Put the flour, salt and black pepper into a large polythene bag and add the chunks of venison. Close the bag and shake, to coat each bit of meat with seasoned flour.

Heat the oil in a large casserole and brown the floured meat, a small amount at a time, browning on all sides. As the venison browns, lift it into a bowl, leaving behind as much oil as possible in the casserole.

When all of the meat is browned, add the finely sliced onions to the casserole and fry, over a moderately high heat, for 8–10 minutes until soft and transparent. As you stir them occasionally during their frying time, scrape the bottom of the pan with your wooden spoon. Replace the browned venison in the casserole with the fried onions and add the ale and stock, stirring continuously. When the liquid reaches simmering point, cover the casserole with its lid and cook in a moderate oven (180°C / 350°F/ gas 4) for 1 hour. Take the casserole out of the oven and cool.

Serves 6

900g / 2lb venison cut into chunks about 2cm / 1", trimmed of any membrane

1 rounded tbsp flour

1 tsp salt, about 15 grinds black pepper

4–5 tbsp olive or rapeseed oil

6 onions, skinned and finely sliced

1 bottle of ale of your choice

300ml / ½ pint stock (I use vegetable stock for this)

Salt and pepper to taste

1 packet all-butter puff pastry, rolled out

1 beaten egg –for brushing the pastry before baking

When it is still warm, taste and add more salt and pepper if you think it is required. Spoon the contents of the casserole into an ovenproof dish or pie dish. Put an inverted eggcup in the middle to support the pastry.

Cover the dish and its contents with the rolled-out puff pastry, and press it down firmly at the sides, making a neat imprint with your thumbs around the edges. With a sharp knife, score the surface of the pastry – take care not to cut right through – into a diamond pattern by cutting lines spaced about 2cm / 1" apart in one way diagonally, then across the other way. Brush the entire surface with beaten egg.

Bake from room temperature (not straight from the fridge) in a moderate oven (180°C / 350°F / gas 4) for 45–50 minutes. The pastry should be golden-brown and puffed and the venison mixture will be simmering gently beneath.

Venison with Red Wine and Marinated Raisins

In this casserole the flavour of the venison is greatly enhanced by the raisins, which are marinated for several hours – or overnight – in red wine. This is an elegant casserole, yet it freezes well and, like all casseroles, it benefits from being cooked, cooled and then reheated carefully before serving. My favourite green vegetable accompaniment for this dish is sliced green beans. And well-beaten buttery mashed potatoes.

Put the raisins, red wine and pared orange rind into a bowl, cover with clingfilm and leave for several hours, or overnight.

Put the flour, salt and black pepper into a large polythene bag and add the chunks of venison. Close the bag and shake, to coat each bit of meat with seasoned flour.

Heat the oil in a casserole and brown the chunks of floured venison, a small amount at a time. As they brown, lift them into a bowl, leaving behind as much oil as you can. When all the venison is browned, reduce the heat slightly beneath the casserole and fry the sliced onions, stirring occasionally, for 5–7 minutes until soft and transparent. Replace the browned meat in amongst the onions, and add the diced garlic and the stock, scraping the base of the casserole as you do so. Add the red wine, raisins and orange rind, and stir until the liquid simmers.

Cover the casserole with its lid and cook in a moderate oven (180°C / 350°F / gas 4) for 1 hour. Take the casserole out of the oven and cool. As it cools, taste and add more salt and black pepper if you think it is needed. Remove the strip of orange rind at this point. When cold, store the casserole in either a cold larder or the fridge.

To serve, bring the casserole into room temperature half an hour before reheating. Reheat on top of the cooker, until the sauce liquid simmers. Then cover the casserole once more and cook, from simmering, in a moderate oven (180°C / 350°F / gas 4) for 20–25 minutes.

Serves 6

900g / 2lb venison, trimmed of any membrane and cut into chunks about 2cm / 1" in size

1 tbsp flour

1 tsp salt, about 15 grinds black pepper

600ml / 1 pint red wine

Pared rind of ½ orange (use a potato peeler to avoid any bitter white pith)

175g / 6oz raisins

4–5 tbsp olive or rapeseed oil

4 onions, skinned and finely sliced

1 fat clove garlic, skinned and finely diced

300ml / ½ pint vegetable stock

Venison Meat Loaf with Roasted Mushroom, Shallot and Crème Fraiche Sauce

Serves 6

For the venison meat loaf

2 onions, skinned and finely diced

4 tbsp olive or rapeseed oil

1 fat clove garlic, skinned and finely diced

900g / 2lb venison leg meat, minced (or briefly whizzed in a processor, a small amount at a time)

1 tsp salt, 20 grinds black pepper

3 tbsp Worcestershire sauce

1 tsp redcurrant jelly

3 large eggs, beaten

2 tbsp finely chopped parsley

I wish I could think of another way to describe this dish without using the words 'meat loaf'! But I can't, so you'll have to believe me when I tell you that it is wonderful. The sauce is extremely good and the two combine to make a delicious lunch or supper, along with accompaniments such as baked jacket potatoes and roast vegetables – carrots, parsnips and leeks is a good combination – to round off the main course.

Line a wide, ovenproof dish about 6cm / 3" deep with baking parchment.

Heat the oil in a wide saucepan and fry the onions, stirring occasionally, for about 5 minutes until soft and transparent. Add the diced garlic just before the frying time is up. Take the pan off the heat and cool the contents.

Put the Worcestershire sauce and redcurrant jelly into a small saucepan over gentle heat. Warm the sauce until the jelly melts. Cool.

Put the minced or pulverised venison into a mixing bowl. Add the cooled fried onions and garlic. Add the cooled Worcestershire sauce and redcurrant jelly combination. Add the salt, black pepper and chopped parsley, and lastly add the beaten eggs. The only way to mix everything together thoroughly is by hand, so make sure that they are scrupulously clean!

When everything is thoroughly amalgamated, put the mixture into the parchment-lined ovenproof dish. Smooth the surface even, cover with parchment – to prevent a crust forming during baking – and cook in a moderate oven (180°C / 350°F / gas 4) for 1½ hours. Take it out of the oven, let it stand for 15 minutes, the dish and its contents loosely covered with foil. Then remove the foil and top parchment, and invert the 'loaf' onto a warmed serving dish. Or if you prefer you can cut and serve it straight from the dish. Any leftovers are very good eaten cold.

Roasted Mushroom, Shallot and Crème Fraiche Sauce

Line a roasting tin with a sheet of baking parchment – this is to make washing-up easier. Put the mushrooms and shallots on to this, with the olive oil, salt and black pepper. With your hands, rub the oil through the mushrooms and shallots, then spread them in an even layer and roast in a hot oven (200°C / 400°F / gas 6) for 35 minutes. Take the roasting tin out of the oven and shuffle around the contents, spread evenly again, and roast for a further 10 minutes.

Take the tin from the oven, and tip the contents into a saucepan. Add the crème fraiche and heat together over moderate heat. Taste, and add more salt and black pepper if you think it is required. Serve hot, spooned over or at the side of each serving of venison meat loaf.

For the roasted mushroom, shallot and crème fraiche sauce

Serves 6

450g / 1lb flat mushrooms, stalks removed, the caps diced to about thumbnail size

3 tbsp olive oil

4 banana shallots, skinned and diced

2 tubs full-fat crème fraiche

1 tsp salt, about 15 grinds black pepper

Braised Venison Kidney with Orange, Tomato and Vermouth

Serves 6

900g / 2lbs kidney, weighed when trimmed and cut into even sized bits approx. 2cms / 1" in size mixed with

2 level tbsp flour

3 onions, each skinned, halved and finely sliced

6 rashers of unsmoked back bacon, sliced into thin strips

3–4 tbsp olive or rapeseed oil

Finely grated rind of 1 orange

1 tbsp tomato puree stirred into

750ml / 1 ¼ pints stock – I use vegetable stock for this

150ml / ¼ pint red Vermouth

1 tsp salt, about 20 grinds of black pepper

Venison kidney is like ox kidney in that it requires lengthy braising, rather than flash frying. The flavours of orange, tomato and the red vermouth go very well with the taste of the kidney. Trimming the kidneys is easier done with a sharp pair of scissors rather than using a knife. This dish is so good eaten with a steamed green vegetable such as Brussels sprouts, and well-beaten mashed potatoes containing horseradish.

Heat the oil in a casserole and brown the floured bits of venison kidney well on all sides. Scoop them into a warm dish and fry the finely sliced onions in the casserole, stirring from time to time so that they cook evenly. When they are transparent – about 5 minutes' cooking – add the finely grated orange rind, the tomato puree and stock, stirring all the time and scraping the bottom of the casserole to mix in the bits on the base of the pan, and stir until the sauce simmers. Add the Vermouth, salt and black pepper, and replace the browned bits of kidney. Cover the casserole with its lid, and cook in a moderate heat (350°F / 180°C / gas mark 4) for 1 hour.

This dish is best eaten after its initial cooking, unlike other casseroles, which benefit from being cooked twice before eating.

INDEX